STECK-VAUGHN

DEVELOPING READING Strategies

EDITORIAL CONSULTANTS

Mary Sue Dillingofski, Ph.D.
Reading Specialist
Educational Consultant
Chicago, Illinois

James P. Menconi
Reading Specialist
Chicago Public Schools
Chicago, Illinois

Betty Willis, Ph.D.
K-12 Reading Specialist
Cypress - Fairbanks School District
Houston, Texas

Summits

Project Design and Development: E.L. Wheetley & Associates, Inc.
Cover Design and Development: D. Childress
Cover Photography: © Bill Ross/West Light

DEVELOPING READING STRATEGIES is a series of six titles listed in recommended sequence:

Challenges
Quests
Ventures
Insights
SUMMITS
Horizons

Published by

STECK-VAUGHN
C O M P A N Y
A Subsidiary of National Education Corporation

Printed in the United States of America.

ISBN 0-8114-5858-X

6 7 8 9 0   C   99 98 97 96 95

CONTENTS

Flying

Read and learn about flying

Wilbur and Orville Wright were bicycle makers in Ohio. They wanted to fly the world's first powered airplane. They began by studying gliders. First they read about a German man who made hundreds of flights in a glider. Next they built their own wind tunnel and used it to learn how to control a glider. Then they tested other aircraft in the tunnel. Finally they built their own engine. On December 17, 1903, after four years of work, they launched their plane. It was buffeted about during a flight that lasted 12 seconds. The age of powered flight had begun.

What do you already know about flying?

Talk about what you know. Get together with a group of students to talk about what you already know about flying. Here are some questions to help you get started.
1. Have people always wanted to fly?
2. What movies have you seen about flying? Have you learned anything from them?
3. How fast can airplanes fly?

Write about what you know. If you could pilot any kind of aircraft, what would you fly? Would you fly a glider, blimp, propeller plane, fighter, airline jet, helicopter, or seaplane? Tell why you made this choice.

_____

_____

_____

_____

Make predictions

Read the titles of the articles in this cluster and look at the picture on page 5. Write three things that you think you'll learn about by reading these articles about flying.

1._____

2._____

3._____

Start to learn new word meanings

All the words listed below are used in the paragraph at the
top of page 4. Study the meanings of these words as you
read about flying.

glider—an aircraft without an engine. *The glider pilot
gently landed the plane in the field.*

launch—push out or put forth into the air. *The crew
prepared to launch the planes from the aircraft carrier.*

buffet—knock about, strike, or hurt. *Strong winds can
buffet a small plane from side to side.*

Learn new skills and strategies

An important strategy you will learn about in this cluster
is making predictions. When you make predictions, you
make good guesses about what you will learn in an article.
You use what you've read and what you already know to
make predictions. Some other skills that you will learn
about in this cluster are finding main ideas and drawing
conclusions.

Gather new information

By the end of this cluster, you will have learned the
answers to these questions.

1. What old Greek myth tells how a man and his son flew?
2. What made Charles Lindbergh a hero around the world?
3. Who is the most famous woman pilot in history?
4. What keeps hang gliders in the air?
5. What pilot was the first to fly faster than the speed of
    sound?

The Flight of Icarus

What do you already know?

Write down three things that you already know about ancient Greek gods and myths. Work with a partner, if you like.

1. _____

2. _____

3. _____

Make predictions

Look at the pictures in the story. Then write two things that you think you'll learn about as you read this story.

1. _____

2. _____

Set your purpose for reading

Write down one thing you hope to find out as you read the story.

_____

_____

Learn important words

Study the meanings of the words below and how they are used in sentences. Knowing these words might help you as you read this story.

craftsman—an artist or a worker in a skilled trade, such as woodworking. *The king always hired the finest craftsmen to work for him.*

labyrinth—a place that has many passageways and blind alleys; a maze. *No one could find his or her way out of the labyrinth on the island.*

soar—fly at a great height; fly upward. *Before the invention of the airplane, only birds could soar.*

An ancient Greek myth tells the story of Daedalus. He was the first great craftsman and engineer. His most famous work was a labyrinth on the island of Crete. According to the myth, angry gods had caused the queen of Crete to give birth to a monster. It was half man and half bull. The king of Crete brought Daedalus to his island to plan a prison for the monster. Daedalus built a labyrinth with so many passages that the monster could never escape.

After finishing his work, Daedalus prepared to return to Greece. The king, however, would not let him go. He knew Daedalus could build many other things for him. Being king of an island, he easily kept Daedalus from leaving by searching all ships before they left Crete.

Using skills and strategies

Making predictions

When you make a prediction, you think ahead. You base your prediction on what has already happened. You also use your knowledge of what usually happens in a situation. A weather forecaster, for example, knows what usually happens when a weather front moves through your area. This knowledge helps the forecaster predict if it will rain.

Think of what has happened so far in this story. Daedalus has been brought in to do a job. He has finished his job and wants to leave. The king doesn't want him to leave. What do you suppose a clever man like Daedalus will do?

Write your prediction in the margin. Then continue reading the story to see if you are right.

The king gave Daedalus a fine workshop at the top of a high tower, but the craftsman wasn't happy. More than anything, he liked to wander wherever he pleased and gather new ideas. Daedalus saw that he could not escape by ship. So he formed a new plan. He would escape by air!

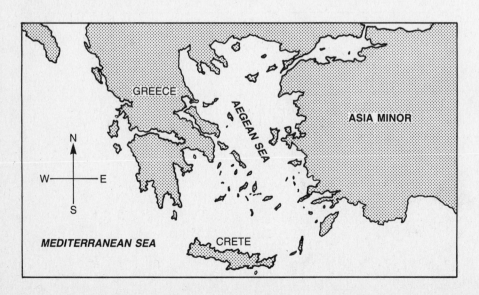

Daedalus studied the wings of birds. Then he designed a set of wings that could support a man. His son, Icarus, was with him on Crete. He asked the boy to gather all the feathers on the island. Because thousands of gulls soared above Crete, the workshop was soon filled with feathers.

Next Daedalus made a wooden frame shaped like the wings of a bird. He pressed melted wax onto the frame. Into the wax he pressed feathers. Finally the wings were finished. Daedalus fastened the wings to his shoulders. He found himself lifted up by the wind. Now sure of his plan, Daedalus made a second pair of wings for Icarus.

Daedalus believed that he and Icarus could jump from the tower and fly across the water. When Icarus' wings were ready, Daedalus gave his son some advice. "If you fly too low, the fog and spray will clog your wings. If you fly too high, the heat of the sun will melt the wax that holds the wings together. Stay near me and you will be safe."

Daedalus fastened the boy's wings to his shoulders. Then both father and son jumped off the tower and began to fly. From time to time, Daedalus looked back to see that his boy was safe. Icarus was feeling the thrill of soaring in the sky like a god. He soared higher and higher until he reached the clouds. Daedalus saw him rising and called out in alarm. He tried to reach the boy, but being heavier, he could not fly that high.

Using skills and strategies

Making predictions

Often, as you read or hear a story, you make a prediction about how the story will end. Later you compare your ending with the ending that the storyteller provided.

This is a good place to predict what will happen to Icarus. Think about the advice that Daedalus gave Icarus. Think about Icarus' behavior so far on his flight. Write your prediction in the margin. Explain why you think your prediction will happen.

Up and up Icarus soared, through the clouds and then above them. He forgot everything except the freedom of flying. The sun beat down on his wings and softened their wax. One by one the feathers loosened and floated down to the sea. Suddenly Icarus began to sink. He flapped his arms wildly, but there were no feathers left. Icarus cried out to his father as he fell toward the waters of the sea.

Daedalus, hearing the boy's cries, called to him. But just then he saw his son falling through the clouds into the sea. Daedalus tried to catch him, but he was too late. He pulled the boy's still body from the sea and flew to land. Weeping bitterly, the father buried his small son.

Then, with a flutter of wings, Daedalus took to the air. When he arrived on land, he built a temple to Apollo, the god of sunlight. In it, Daedalus hung his wings as an offering to the god. And he mourned for his son.

Think About What You've Read

Important ideas

1. Why did Daedalus have to fly to leave Crete?

_____

_____

2. What warning did Daedalus give Icarus about flying high?

_____

_____

3. If you had been at the tower when Daedalus and Icarus began their flight, what advice would you have given them?

_____

_____

4. How can you tell that this story is not true?

_____

_____

Use what you've learned before

5. Stories that have been popular since ancient times are based on feelings people have always had and still have. What are some of these feelings in "The Flight of Icarus"?

_____

_____

9

Important word meanings

Think about the meaning of each word listed below. Below each word, write words or phrases that come to your mind as you think of it. Write at least three words or phrases for each vocabulary word.

craftsman	labyrinth	soar
_____	_____	_____
_____	_____	_____
_____	_____	_____
_____	_____	_____
_____	_____	_____

Using skills and strategies

Do you think that Daedalus ever made new wings to fly again? Give a reason for your prediction.

_____

_____

_____

_____

Writing

Flying was the most exciting experience of Icarus's life. Recall the most exciting moments of your life. Choose one that you wish to share. On a separate sheet of paper, describe the moment. Try to let your readers feel what you felt at that time.

Your important ideas

Look back over the story. Write down one idea that seems to be the most important one to you—the one idea that you would like to remember.

_____

_____

Your important words

Look back at the words you have learned as you read about the flight of Icarus. Write down the word or words that you think are most important—that you would like to remember.

_____

_____

Lucky Lindy

What do you already know?

Write down three things that you already know about airplanes and flying in the early years of this century. Work with a partner, if you like.

1. _____

2. _____

3. _____

Make predictions

Look at the pictures and the headings, the words in large type in the article. Then write down three things that you think you'll learn about as you read this article.

1. _____

2. _____

3. _____

Set your purpose for reading

Write down one thing you hope to find out about Charles Lindbergh's flight as you read this article.

_____

_____

Learn important words

Study the meanings of the words below and how they are used in sentences. Knowing these words might help you as you read this article.

transatlantic—crossing or extending across the Atlantic Ocean. *Charles Lindbergh made the first solo transatlantic crossing in an airplane from New York to Paris.*

aviator—person who flies an aircraft; pilot. *Pilots of airplanes, helicopters, or balloons are aviators.*

design—an outline, sketch, or plan, as of some product; the combination of features of the plan. *Aircraft builders steadily improved the design of the wings.*

In 1919, two Englishmen were the first to fly across the Atlantic Ocean. They flew the shortest possible route. They took off from the east coast of Newfoundland and landed on the west coast of Ireland.

The challenge

As soon as the Englishmen landed, a Frenchman issued a greater challenge. Raymond Orteig offered $25,000 to the first aviator to cross the Atlantic where it was much wider. His prize would go to the flier who traveled nonstop between New York and Paris.

For years, no one attempted to win the prize. Pilots knew their planes couldn't fly that great a distance.

Using skills and strategies

Main ideas

You will understand what you read if you keep track of the most important ideas. Here's how. After reading a paragraph, ask "What was the paragraph about?" All three paragraphs above are about flying. Flying is the topic.

After you decide what the topic is, ask "What is the most important thing I learned about the topic?" In the second paragraph, the most important idea is that Raymond Orteig offered $25,000 to the first aviator to fly between New York and Paris. This is the main idea of the paragraph. The other sentences in the paragraph give details that explain and support the main idea.

In many paragraphs, one sentence states the main idea. In paragraph 3, circle the sentence that states the main idea. Underline the sentence that supports the main idea.

As time went on, airplanes improved. Aviators decided it was possible to try for the prize. In September of 1926, a French pilot and three crewmen attempted a transatlantic flight. However, their plane carried so much fuel that its three engines couldn't lift it off the ground. It crashed on takeoff, killing two crewmen. This crash, however, did not stop other people from trying. Within months, at least six teams in the United States and Europe were planning flights for the spring.

Lindbergh enters the race

Late in 1926, a young American aviator, Charles Lindbergh, dreamed of being the first to cross the ocean. But he didn't have the money to build a transatlantic plane. Some business people in St. Louis, Missouri, agreed to support him. In February, Lindbergh found a tiny California airline company that would build him a plane in two months. The young pilot named his plane the *Spirit of St. Louis.*

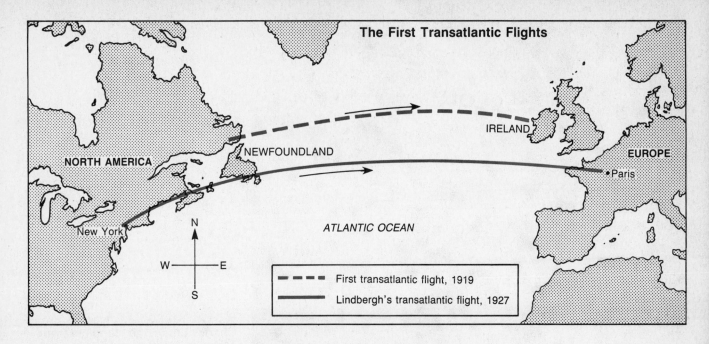

The First Transatlantic Flights

NORTH AMERICA

NEWFOUNDLAND

IRELAND

EUROPE

Paris

New York

ATLANTIC OCEAN

N
W — E
S

- - - - First transatlantic flight, 1919
———— Lindbergh's transatlantic flight, 1927

Lindbergh worked with the engineers on the design of the plane. Together they decided on the size of the engine and of the wings, the placement of the gas tank, and all the other details. Lindbergh also worked out the details of his flight. He would fly alone. This would allow him to take more fuel. His instruments would keep him on course.

After 60 days, the *Spirit of St. Louis* was ready. In early May, Lindbergh flew the plane from San Diego to New York City. Then he waited for good weather over the Atlantic. Finally, at 6 P.M. on May 19, the New York Weather Bureau gave a promising report. The North Atlantic was clearing, with only small storms on the coast of Europe. Lindbergh went to the airfield and prepared his plane. He tried to nap, but he was too tense to sleep.

33 hours to glory

During the time the *Spirit of St. Louis* was being built, three planes attempted transatlantic flights. All had crashed or disappeared over the ocean, killing seven aviators. Two other aircraft were almost ready to attempt the crossing. The other planes were larger, with two-man crews and rich backers. Lindbergh was flying his tiny plane alone and didn't have much money.

Reports about all the fliers appeared in newspapers all over the country. People rooted for Lindbergh because he seemed to have little chance of succeeding. It seemed the whole nation was hoping Lindbergh would be "lucky."

Lindbergh, however, was not waiting for luck. The quiet man knew everything there was to know about his plane. He had planned his flight as carefully as possible. Now he returned to the airfield before daybreak and studied the flying conditions.

Charles Lindbergh stands in front of the plane he flew on his record flight.

The dirt runway was muddy. This might slow the plane down as it tried to take off. Telephone wires stood at the end of the runway. If the plane was not high enough when it reached them, it would crash into the wires.

The airplane was heavy. This was to be the first time that the gasoline tanks were completely filled. No other engine the size of Lindbergh's had lifted this much weight.

If the wind was blowing in the right direction, it could help lift the plane off the runway. It wasn't. Should Lindbergh wait for better conditions? He made his decision. The builders and his supporters had done their jobs. Now he had to do his.

Using skills and strategies

Main idea

The next paragraph states the main idea in one sentence. Underline the sentence that states the main idea.

A little after 7:30 A.M. on May 20, the young aviator started his engine. The silver-colored plane crept slowly down the runway. Then it began picking up speed and the wings began to lift. The *Spirit of St. Louis* took off. The slightest mistake would send it plunging back to Earth. Lindbergh climbed slowly. Then he steadied the wings and pulled the nose higher. The little plane barely cleared the telephone wires! Cheering loudly, the airport crowd watched the plane disappear into the sky. Word of the flight was sent around the world: "Lindbergh is on his way."

After two hours, the *Spirit of St. Louis* had passed the Massachusetts coast, heading northeast. Then Lindbergh crossed Nova Scotia. From then on, only ocean lay below.

Lindbergh's flight became a battle against his need to sleep. There were periods of danger—fog, sleet, changes in air speed. Lindbergh was instantly alert during signs of trouble. But as soon as he solved the problems, his body again ached for sleep.

Over the ocean, day passed into night, and night passed into the second day. Lindbergh flew with the windows open so that the cold air would keep him awake. Looking below, he saw porpoises in the water and a few birds. Then, after 27 hours of flying, Lindbergh spotted black dots on the water. Flying lower, he saw that they were boats. Land could not be far away! An hour passed, and then Lindbergh sighted the coast of Ireland!

Wide awake now, Lindbergh soared over England and on to France. Soon he was flying over Paris to the airfield just outside the city. On May 21, 1927, Charles Lindbergh landed the *Spirit of St. Louis* in Paris. The quiet young aviator was greeted by cheering crowds. He was now a hero around the world. Lindbergh had shown courage, desire for adventure, understanding of machines, and great skill in flying. Charles Lindbergh became the most famous flier of that age.

Think About What You've Read

Important ideas

1. Why didn't pilots try to win the Orteig prize when it was first offered in 1919?

2. How did Lindbergh help design the *Spirit of St. Louis?*

3. Do you think Lindbergh deserved all the attention and fame he won? Give reasons for your answer.

Use what you've learned before

4. What is one difference between the stories of Icarus and Charles Lindbergh?

Important word meanings

Many words or word parts come from words in other languages. All the words below come from the *Latin* language. Match the Latin words and their meanings in column 2 with the words in column 1. Write the letter of the answer next to each numeral.

Column 1	Column 2
_____ 1. aviator	a. Latin *designare*, "to mark out"
_____ 2. design	b. Latin *trans-*, "across"
_____ 3. soar	c. Latin *avi-*, "bird"
_____ 4. transatlantic	d. Latin *aura*, "air"

Using skills and strategies

Reread the paragraph on page 14 beginning "The dirt runway." Its main idea is not stated. In other words, none of the sentences in the paragraph tells the main idea. Write the main idea, in your own words, on the lines below.

_____

_____

_____

Writing

Think of a time you had to do something difficult by yourself. On a separate sheet of paper, describe your experience. Explain how you overcame the difficulties.

Your important ideas

Look back over the article. Write down one idea that seems to be the most important one to you—the one idea that you would like to remember.

_____

_____

Your important words

Look back at the words you have learned as you read about Charles Lindbergh. Write down the word or words that you think are most important—that you would like to remember.

_____

_____

Amelia Earhart's Last Flight

What do you already know?

Write down three things that you already know about famous early aviators. Work with a partner, if you like.

1. _____

2. _____

3. _____

Make predictions

Look at the pictures in the article. Then write down three things that you think you'll learn about as you read this article.

1. _____

2. _____

3. _____

Set your purpose for reading

Write down one thing you hope to find out about Amelia Earhart as you read this article.

_____

_____

Learn important words

Study the meanings of the words below and how they are used in sentences. Knowing these words might help you as you read this article.

navigator—one who determines the position, path, and distance traveled by a ship or airplane. *The navigator determined the position of the airplane.*

antenna—a rod or wire for sending and receiving radio waves. *A long antenna will receive weak signals better.*

solo—alone. *Charles Lindbergh made the first solo flight from New York to Paris.*

By 1932, thousands of women across the world had become airplane pilots. One of the best known was a friendly, independent young woman from Kansas, Amelia Earhart. In 1928, Amelia was the first woman to make a transatlantic flight—as a passenger. In 1932, she became the first woman to fly solo across the Atlantic. Three years later Amelia made a flight that no male pilot had yet achieved—a solo flight from Hawaii to California.

Amelia drew many other women into flying because of her successes and her charm as a public figure. In 1935, she went into teaching, to advise young fliers. Still, she wanted to make one final long-distance flight. She would fly around the world at the Equator—27,000 miles! With the zig-zags needed for fueling stops, the trip would be about 29,000 miles all together. A few pilots had followed a shorter path north of the Equator, but no one had attempted the trip Earhart planned.

Preparing for the flight took almost a year. Finally, everything was ready. On March 17, 1937, Amelia's twin-engine plane took off heading west from California. Less than 16 hours later, she landed in Hawaii. The plane was refueled and tested.

The next day Amelia and her two navigators headed down the runway. At once she knew something was wrong. The aircraft did not gain enough speed to take off. A wing dropped. Then the landing gear failed, and the plane spun off the runway. The landing gear and wing were smashed.

Amelia knew there would be a long delay for repairs. This meant the plane would be flying over the Caribbean in the middle of the rainy season. The stormy weather would be too dangerous to fly through. Amelia decided to reverse her direction and head east along the Equator. This way she'd pass over the Caribbean at the start of the trip.

Using skills and strategies

Drawing conclusions

To draw a conclusion, you make a decision based on facts. In the paragraph above, Amelia Earhart concluded that she should reverse the direction of her flight. She based her conclusion on these facts.

1. Plane repairs forced a change in schedule that would take her into the Caribbean during the rainy season.
2. It was too dangerous to fly through the Caribbean during the rainy season.
3. Reversing the direction of her flight would take her over the Caribbean before the rainy season.

The paragraph that follows tells how Earhart concluded she should leave her plane's antenna behind. Underline the facts that led to this conclusion.

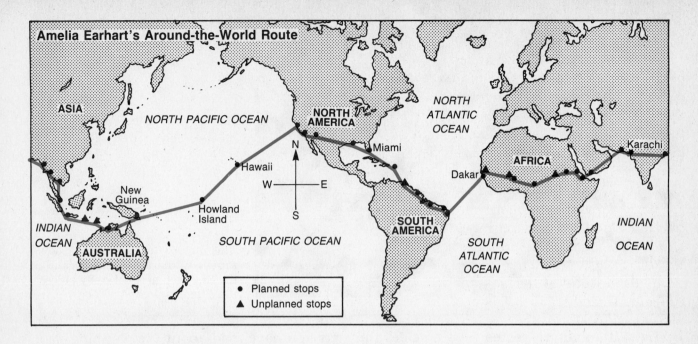

Amelia Earhart's Around-the-World Route

• Planned stops
▲ Unplanned stops

Amelia's plane was put on a ship and taken back to California for repairs. Then she and one remaining navigator, Fred Noonan, flew the first leg of the flight to Miami, Florida. More repairs were made in Miami. The radio repairmen there couldn't get her radio to work properly. They told Amelia that the 250-foot antenna for her emergency radio was causing the trouble. They said she didn't need it. So Earhart decided to leave the antenna in Miami.

On June 1, Amelia again took off. During the next month, she and Fred Noonan made an amazing journey. (With a pencil, trace the journey on the map above.) They flew south from Miami to South America and east across the continent. From Brazil, they crossed 1,900 miles of ocean to Dakar, Africa. From Dakar they flew across the Sahara Desert and on to Karachi, India. There they took time to sightsee and ride a camel. Next, the two flew through Southeast Asia and to Australia. On July 1, after flying 22,000 miles, Earhart and Noonan landed in New Guinea.

The next part of the flight would be the longest and most dangerous. Amelia had chosen a route no one had ever flown. She would fly more than 2,500 miles over open water, and land on Howland Island. Howland is a tiny speck in the ocean. If Noonan and Earhart mistook their position by only one degree on their compass, they would miss the island.

At 10 A.M. on July 2, the plane lifted off from the jungle airstrip. A U.S. ship, the *Itasca*, was in the water off Howland Island. Amelia was due at Howland about 6:30 A.M. the following morning. If she wasn't there by dawn, the ship would send up smoke signals to help her find the island.

This picture, taken in 1929, shows Amelia Earhart after she became the first woman pilot to fly across the Atlantic Ocean.

Using skills and strategies

Drawing conclusions

Consider the facts you have read about the planning for this trip and events so far on the trip. Which of these conclusions would you draw?
1. *Amelia's flight had reasonable chances of success.*
2. *Amelia's flight had almost no chance of success.*

Review the article and underline facts that support either conclusion. Then circle the conclusion you draw.

At 6:15 A.M., Amelia's voice came over the *Itasca*'s radio. She thought she was about 200 miles away and asked what her position was. There was too much static on the radio for the *Itasca* to answer. The *Itasca* asked Amelia to stay on the air longer, but there was no reply.

Amelia's planned arrival time came and went, but her plane did not appear. Half an hour after her arrival time, Amelia radioed the *Itasca* asking for her location. The signal was strong, so her plane was close by. But Amelia left the air too soon for the men to figure out where she was. They sent messages asking her to answer on her emergency radio. They didn't know that her emergency radio was useless because its antenna had been left in Miami.

At 7:42 A.M., Amelia's voice came in strong. "We must be on you but cannot see you," she said. "But gas is running low. Been unable to reach you by radio. We are flying at altitude 1,000 feet." The men on the *Itasca* called Amelia and told her they'd received her signal. They asked her again to reply on the emergency radio.

Six minutes later, Amelia's voice came in clearly again. She sounded troubled. She had not heard any of their messages. The men radioed to her again and again.

A few minutes after 8:00 A.M., Amelia told them that she had heard their signals for the first time. Still, she couldn't find land. The *Itasca* kept sending signals begging her to answer. The plane was two hours late. The *Itasca* was sending smoke signals to guide Amelia. But there was no plane heading for the island.

The next message from Amelia came through at 8:45 A.M. She sounded upset. The signal was the strongest one she'd sent. Surely her plane was close to Howland. The men on the ship kept calling her. Minutes dragged by. They listened on the radio but heard nothing. The men realized that by now Amelia was out of fuel. The plane must have crashed.

The *Itasca* searched the water near Howland. Several other U.S. Navy ships and planes joined the search. After sixteen days, they had covered more than 250,000 square miles of ocean. They found nothing.

Americans couldn't believe that Amelia was dead. In 1937, Japanese-American relations were tense. Some Americans thought that Amelia had been sent on a secret mission to photograph the Japanese islands. Could Amelia have been taken prisoner? It seemed easier to accept that than her death. Less than two years later, World War II broke out. Years passed, and still Amelia's disappearance was not solved.

Books about Amelia's disappearance continue to be written. But the mystery may never be solved. From her messages, it would seem that she crashed into the ocean when the plane ran out of fuel. We know for certain only of her courage, for which she is still admired today.

Think About What You've Read

Important ideas

1. What was Amelia Earhart trying to accomplish on her last flight?

2. After planning the flight for a year, why did Amelia have to change all her plans?

3. Suppose that the Miami radio repairmen had not told Amelia that she didn't need her emergency antenna. Do you think her flight would have been any different? Give reasons for your conclusion.

4. Name an improvement made in airplanes and air travel between Lindbergh's transatlantic flight and Amelia's last flight.

_____

_____

Important word meanings

Underline sentences in the article that use each of these words: *attempt, aviator, navigator, solo,* and *antenna*. Then, on a separate sheet of paper, write a few sentences about Amelia Earhart that use all five words.

Using skills and strategies

No one knows for certain what happened to Earhart and Noonan. One possibility is that they died as prisoners of the Japanese. What evidence suggests this is unlikely? List information from this article and its map that leads you to the conclusion that they were not taken prisoner.

_____

_____

_____

Writing

Imagine that you are a newspaper reporter at the time Amelia Earhart took her around-the-world flight. On a separate sheet of paper, write an article about the flight for your newspaper. You may wish to write straight news and report just the facts. If you prefer, write an article giving your opinions of the events. Give your article a headline that will make others want to read it.

Your important ideas

Look back over the article. Write down one idea that seems to be the most important one to you—the one idea that you would like to remember.

_____

_____

Your important words

Look back at the words you have learned as you read about Amelia Earhart. Write down the word or words that you think are most important—that you would like to remember.

_____

_____

Hang Gliding

What do you already know?

Write down three things that you already know about hang gliding. Work with a partner, if you like.

1. _____

2. _____

3. _____

Make predictions

Look at the picture in the article. Skim the text briefly. That is, look it over quickly for words or ideas that are easy to notice. Then write three things that you think you'll learn about as you read this article.

1. _____

2. _____

3. _____

Set your purpose for reading

Write down one thing you hope to find out about hang gliding as you read this article.

_____

_____

Learn important words

Study the meanings of the words below and how they are used in sentences. Knowing these words might help you as you read this article.

glider—an aircraft without a motor. *Rising air currents kept the glider up in the air.*

launch—push out or put forth into the air. *Pilots launch some gliders by pulling them forward with cars or motor boats.*

maneuver—to move skillfully. *A hang-glider pilot can maneuver in the air for hours.*

thermal—a rising current of warm air. *A glider can gain altitude by flying into a thermal.*

Hang gliding is the closest humans come to flying like birds. Gliding is flying without an engine. In hang gliding, pilots hang below the glider wings on a swing seat or in a harness.

How does hang gliding work? In most ways, it works like other types of aircraft. Air meeting the glider's wing breaks into two parts. The part that goes over the wing's curved upper surface must travel faster than the wind that goes below. This causes the air pressure above the wing to be less than the air below the wing. The air then pushes upward, and it naturally pushes the wing up, too. This effect is called *lift*. The faster the wind is moving across a wing, the more lift the wing gets. When a glider or plane gets enough lift, it will fly.

To launch themselves, hang-glider pilots often step off cliffs or leap from mountains. The gliders pick up speed as they fall. The gliders quickly level off because air flowing past the wings gives them lift. If the pilots steer the gliders into strong air currents, the gliders can stay in the air a long time.

Using skills and strategies

Using a dictionary

As you read, you will come across words for which the meaning is not clear. Sometimes sentences around a word help you figure out its meaning. If they do not, you'll need to look up the word in a dictionary.

To help you understand the second paragraph in the article, look up *air pressure*. It will be under the first word, *air*. Write *air pressure* and its meaning in the margin on this page.

As you continue to read the article, circle words that you don't know. When you are finished, look up the words that are still unclear. Then reread the article for better understanding.

Pilots maneuver hang gliders by shifting their own weight. Shifting the weight changes the center of gravity on the hang glider. From then on, gravity pulls from the direction of the pilot's new position. To turn right, for example, a pilot moves his or her body toward the right.

If the air is perfectly still, the lift on the glider wings will be less than the weight of glider and pilot. The flight will last only a few moments. Therefore, to stay in the air, pilots must find air that is in motion. One way to find wind is to look for landforms, such as hills or cliffs. Such forms force the air moving along the ground to rise upward. The pilot must be careful to maneuver the glider to the side of the landform where the air moves up. To be on the opposite side, in downward air, is dangerous.

Pilots often launch their hang gliders by stepping off the sides of cliffs.

Using skills and strategies

Using a dictionary

A dictionary provides other information in addition to the meaning of a word. Look up one of the words you circled. Write your word in the margin. Then, under the word, write the hyphenation and pronunciation you find in the dictionary. Here is an example of the hyphenation and pronunciation of the word *maneuver*.

hyphenation (how to split a word into syllables) ma neu ver

pronunciation (how to say a word) muh NOO vuhr

Thermals are among hang gliders' favorite air currents. The air in them is rising. Many hang-glider pilots try to find thermals so they can stay in the air a long time. Since thermals are limited in size, pilots circle around and around in them. A pilot who rides a thermal to a high altitude before gliding down will fall gently for a long distance.

There are only a few ways to find thermals. One is to look for clouds. When a thermal with some moisture in its air rises high enough, the moisture forms clouds. Another way is to watch soaring birds. Many birds fly upward in spiraling patterns to feed on insects carried by thermals. Some pilots learn to smell thermals. If they smell something from the ground when they are flying high above it, they know they are flying through a thermal.

The most difficult maneuver of a flight is the landing. Launches are easier because pilots have time to think things through. In a landing, however, pilots have only seconds in which to figure out what to do and then do it. Good pilots attempt to make their glider stop moving at the same moment their feet touch the ground.

Think About What You've Read

Important ideas

1. How do an aircraft's wings help keep it in the air?

_____

_____

2. Do you think hang gliding can be dangerous? Why or why not?

_____

_____

_____

Use what you've learned before
3. Which came first, gliders or powered airplanes? How do you know?

_____

_____

Important word meanings
   Use all five of these words in a brief paragraph about hang gliders. Write on a separate sheet of paper.

   glider   launch   maneuver   soar   thermal

Using skills and strategies
   Find the word *lift* in a dictionary. Write the meaning for the way *lift* is used in this article.

_____

_____

Writing
   Hang gliding is a sport that requires skill. Think of a sport you play. Write a paragraph that describes the skills needed for your sport. Use a separate sheet of paper.

Your important ideas
   Look back over the article. Write down one idea that seems to be the most important one to you.

_____

Your important words
   Look back at the words you have learned as you read about hang gliding. Write down the word or words that you think are most important.

_____

Breaking the Sound Barrier

What do you already know?

Write down three things that you think you already know about flying faster than the speed of sound. Work with a partner, if you like.

1. _____

2. _____

3. _____

Make predictions

Look at the picture and the headings in the article. Then write down three things that you think you'll learn about as you read this article.

1. _____

2. _____

3. _____

Set your purpose for reading

Write down one thing you hope to find out about breaking the sound barrier as you read this article.

_____

_____

Learn important words

Study the meanings of the words below and how they are used in sentences. Knowing these words might help you as you read this article.

instrument—a tool for measuring, recording, or controlling. *A thermometer is an instrument for measuring temperature.*

buffet—to knock about or strike; to struggle. *Strong winds can buffet a small plane from side to side.*

supersonic—greater than the speed of sound in air. *Planes need powerful engines to reach supersonic speeds.*

When the planes used in World War II were flown at high speeds, they began to shake wildly. Some of these planes didn't respond to the controls. Then the motion broke the planes apart, killing their pilots and crews. What was attacking the planes? Was there a barrier in the sky against fast speeds?

The problem with sound waves

Some of the planes that went out of control at high altitudes fell quickly to low altitudes. There, suddenly, they began to respond to controls again. This was the clue the researchers needed. It told them that sound waves were causing the problem.

At sea level, sound travels at 760 miles per hour. Normally, we hear something—such as a low-flying plane—for a while before it comes close to us. The sound waves travel faster than the plane.

Sound waves travel in air like waves in water. But the higher you go, the less air there is. The less air there is, the slower sound travels. At 35,000 feet, sound travels at only 660 miles per hour.

The researchers knew that planes did not travel at 760 miles per hour. But in steep, fast dives, they could reach the speed of sound. The planes were catching up with their own sound waves. They were crashing into their sound waves!

Was there a sound barrier? Would every plane that went as fast as sound be knocked apart by its own sound waves?

Chuck Yeager, an Air Force test pilot, was chosen to fly the plane that would break the sound barrier.

As you know, predicting means making a good guess based on what you know. For example, if you've enjoyed meals at a certain restaurant in the past, you can predict you will enjoy future meals there. But if you've never eaten there, you need other information, such as how well other people have liked meals there. Then you can make a prediction.

The paragraphs on page 28 describe a serious problem. At the time, no one could predict whether the problem could be solved. Can you predict how researchers could get the information they needed? Use what you have learned from the title, headings, and pictures. Write your prediction in the margin. Continue reading to see if your prediction is correct.

Finding the answer

Had flying reached its final speed limit? A special plane called the *X-1* was built to find out. Only 30 feet long, the *X-1* could withstand a tremendous amount of force. Four large rocket engines powered the *X-1*. However, the rockets would not be used for takeoff. Instead, a larger plane would carry the *X-1* up to 25,000 feet and drop it. This would save rocket fuel needed to reach supersonic speeds.

The speed of sound is called Mach 1. Speeds lower than Mach 1 are given as decimal numbers, such as Mach 0.9. At the time the *X-1* was delivered to the U.S. Air Force, it had been flown to Mach 0.8.

In 1947, a 24-year-old West Virginian named Chuck Yeager was chosen to try flying the *X-1* through the sound barrier. Yeager was an Air Force officer. His plane had been shot down over France during World War II. Yeager avoided capture and made his way to Britain. Returning to duty, he shot down twelve enemy planes and was awarded many medals. After the war, Yeager became a test pilot.

Yeager got used to the *X-1* by flying it as a glider, without firing the engine. The plane flew well and glided downward to land on a dried-up lake bed in the desert. Yeager took three unpowered flights. When he finally used the engines, Yeager fired each engine separately. Using three of the four engines, he reached Mach 0.87. He then turned off the engines, and glided down.

The research team wanted to explore the speeds up to Mach 1 gradually. Therefore, the second powered flight was made to Mach 0.89, and the third one to Mach 0.91. On each of these flights, Yeager found it more and more difficult to control the plane. Later research showed this was because supersonic shock waves form on the wings before an aircraft reaches Mach 1.

This happens because air flows over the curved surfaces of a plane at a speed faster than the plane is traveling. As the plane approaches the speed of sound, the airflow becomes uneven. The wings begin to vibrate, causing the plane to buffet. The plane becomes hard to control. All this occurs when the airflow around the airplane has reached the speed of sound before the airplane itself has. This is the "sound barrier."

Yeager flew several more times near Mach 0.9. On each flight, he and the research team learned more about the effects of the sound waves on the plane.

Using skills and strategies

Making predictions

Do you think that Chuck Yeager was afraid that the *X-1* would be destroyed when it approached the sound barrier? Predict whether or not you think the rest of the article will tell you about Yeager's feelings. Write your prediction and the reasons you used to make it in the margin.

On October 14, 1947, the *X-1* was air-launched for the purpose of breaking the sound barrier. Yeager fired all four rocket engines. They pushed the plane to 37,000 feet. Yeager leveled off. His speed increased. The *X-1* began to buffet at Mach 0.86, as shock waves formed on the wings. As the speed increased, the buffeting increased. The worst occurred around Mach 0.93. Then Yeager sped up a bit. He was at Mach 0.97, about to travel into the unknown. Suddenly, the Mach measuring instrument jumped to 1.05! All the buffeting was gone. The supersonic airflow was smooth over the entire airplane. Yeager and the *X-1* had broken the sound barrier!

As practiced many times before, Yeager brought the *X-1* in for a perfect glider landing. This flight opened the way to a new era in air travel—the supersonic age.

Think About What You've Read

Important ideas

1. What were the World War II fighter planes bumping into?

2. Describe how the *X-1* was built to break the sound barrier.

Use what you've learned before

3. Do you think that Lindbergh would have been a good
   test pilot? Why?

_____

_____

Important word meanings

Each word in dark type is followed by two different
meanings. Underline the meaning that describes the word
in dark type. Choose the meaning used in the article.

supersonic	faster than sound	slower than sound
buffet	polish	knock about
instrument	plays music	measures something
launch	land on lake bed	put into the air
aviator	pilot	airplane

Using skills and strategies

Predict what researchers did with the *X-1* after it broke
the sound barrier. Give reasons for your prediction.

_____

_____

_____

Writing

Would you like to be a test pilot? Write a short letter to
Chuck Yeager telling why you would or would not want to
do his job. Order your reasons from least important to most
important. Write on a separate sheet of paper.

Your important ideas

Look back over the article. Write down one idea that
seems to be the most important one to you—the one idea
that you would like to remember.

_____

_____

Your important words

Look back at the words you have learned as you read
about breaking the sound barrier. Write down the word or
words that you think are most important.

_____

_____

Reviewing What You Have Learned

CLUSTER 1

Some facts and ideas you have learned

You learned many important facts and ideas as you read about flying. A few of them are listed below. Add your own important ideas to the end of the list. You can look back at the "Your important ideas" section of each lesson to remember the ideas you wrote down.

- In an old Greek myth, Daedalus escaped from an island by making wings and flying.
- Charles Lindbergh was the first person to fly solo nonstop from New York to Paris.
- Amelia Earhart hoped to fly around the world at the Equator.
- Rising air currents keep hang gliders in the air.
- Chuck Yeager was the pilot who broke the sound barrier.

_____

_____

_____

_____

Some word meanings you have learned

Here are some of the important words you learned in the articles you read. Make sure you understand their meanings. Then add important words of your own. You can look back at the "Your important words" section of each lesson to remember the words you wrote down.

aviator—a person who flies an aircraft; pilot. *Amelia Earhart was a famous aviator who broke many records.*

thermal—a rising current of warm air. *Hang-glider pilots can make long flights by soaring in thermals.*

supersonic—greater than the speed of sound in air. *Some passenger planes can travel at supersonic speeds.*

_____

_____

_____

Purposes for reading

Look back at the sections at the beginning of every lesson called "Set your purposes for reading." Did the articles in this cluster enable you to achieve your purposes? Write one purpose that you felt you did not yet achieve. Tell what other reading you can do to achieve that purpose.

_____

_____

32

Using skills and strategies

Reread the section entitled "The problem with sound waves" on page 28, in the article "Breaking the Sound Barrier." On the lines below, briefly list the facts that led researchers to draw the conclusion that sound waves were destroying fighter planes.

_____

_____

_____

_____

Writing: evaluation

Which aviator—Charles Lindbergh, Amelia Earhart, or Chuck Yeager—do you think was the bravest? Write a paragraph that gives at least two reasons for your choice. Use a separate sheet of paper.

Revising

Read what you wrote. Did you present your ideas in a logical order? Would your paragraph be better if the sentences were arranged in a different order? If so, change the order and rewrite the paper.

Activities

1. Write down the dates of Charles Lindbergh's or Amelia Earhart's flights. Take them to your local library. Ask the librarian to help you find a newspaper article reporting one of these flights. (The Air Force did not report Chuck Yeager's flight at the time it was made.) Make a copy of an article that reports one of the flights and show the article to the class. Tell the class how the article is different from the one in this cluster.
2. Look up *aircraft* in the *Guinness Book of World Records*. Read about other record-breaking flights described there. Tell the class about the ones that interest you.
3. If your class is interested in hang gliding, find out whether there are any hang-gliding clubs in your area. If there are, invite a member to speak to your class about the sport. Have questions ready to ask the speaker. Send a thank-you note to the speaker afterward.
4. Experiment with designing and making paper airplanes. Hold a competition with others who have made paper airplanes to see whose plane will glide the farthest.
5. Rent a copy of the movie *The Right Stuff* at a video store. The first part of the movie tells about Chuck Yeager and the *X-1*. Tell your class about details you learned from the movie that weren't in the article about breaking the sound barrier.

Disasters

Read and learn about disasters

When the space shuttle *Challenger* exploded, millions of people were shocked. We sat glued to the television or radio, following report after report. We asked ourselves how the incident could have happened. Some of us wondered how we would have felt if we had been there. Thinking about the disaster affected our lives.

Severe disasters have always shocked people and made us think about our lives. They remind us that we can't always control the future. They force us to remember what's important in life. They also bring out hidden parts of people. Some people discover their own terror or selfishness. Others find kindness and wisdom they did not know they had. As bad as disasters can be, they can teach us about ourselves.

What do you already know about disasters?

Talk about what you know. Get together with a group of students and talk about what you already know about famous disasters. Here are some questions to help you get started.

1. What causes disasters?
2. What are some famous disasters in history?
3. What can be done to prevent disasters from happening?

Write about what you know. Choose one disaster that you know something about. Write a brief description of what happened. You might write about what caused the disaster, how people acted, or how people recovered.

_____

_____

Make predictions

Read the titles of the articles in this cluster and look at the picture on page 35. Write down three things that you think you'll learn by reading about disasters.

1. _____

2. _____

3. _____

Natural events can create major disasters. The picture shows a hospital destroyed by a 1985 earthquake in Mexico City.

Start to learn new word meanings

All the words listed below are used in the two paragraphs on page 34. Study the meanings of these words as you read about disasters.

incident—an event. *Our search for Martians was an incident I'll never forget.*

severe—very serious. *The severe lack of rainfall caused the crops to die.*

terror—great fear. *We shook with terror when the flames reached our house.*

Learn new skills and strategies

One of the skills you will learn about in this cluster is sequencing. This means putting ideas or events in order as you read. When you do this, you help yourself to remember what you read. You also will learn about self-questioning and taking notes as you read this cluster.

Gather new information

By the end of this cluster, you will have read about the answers to these questions.

1. How did different people act when they were caught in the Great Chicago Fire?
2. In what ways did ancient people live like people today?
3. How could the greatest sea tragedy of all time have been prevented?
4. Why did people panic when they heard a radio play?
5. How can we help end the disaster of famine?

Fire!

What do you already know?

In 1871, a huge fire raged through the city of Chicago. Write down three things you already know about that fire or about fire in general. Work with a partner, if you like.

1. _____

2. _____

3. _____

Make predictions

Look at the pictures and headings in this article. Then write down three facts that you think you will learn as you read the article.

1. _____

2. _____

3. _____

Set your purpose for reading

Write down one thing you hope to find out about the Great Chicago Fire as you read this article.

_____

_____

_____

Learn important words

Study the meanings of the words below and the way they are used in sentences. Knowing these words might help you as you read this article.

terror—great fear. *The people of Chicago would long remember the terror of that awful disaster.*

embers—things glowing with fire; usually pieces of coal or wood. *Hot embers from the fire covered everything in sight.*

vicious—cruel and mean; evil. *The fire was like a vicious animal destroying everything in its path.*

invalid—very sick; a very sick person. *He worried about getting his invalid father out of the building and away from the fire.*

The summer of 1871 was hot and dry in Chicago. Very little rain fell. By fall, the wooden buildings in the city were like firewood. In the first week of October, 20 major fires broke out in Chicago. On October 7, four square blocks of buildings burned. Fire fighters were worn out. They didn't know that the worst was yet to come.

On Sunday evening, October 8, Catherine O'Leary carried her oil lamp to her barn to check on the cows. One of them kicked over the lamp. Oil spilled across the wooden floor and caught fire. The flames spread through the barn, and then strong winds carried the fire outside. The flames jumped quickly from street to street, all through the city. The fire raged for more than 24 hours before it died out. This was the Great Chicago Fire.

At the time of the fire, Alexander Frear was visiting his brother's family in Chicago. When news of the fire came, he was with his sister-in-law and his nephew in one part of the city. His nieces were in another part of the city. Frear and his nephew set out to find the girls. Afterward, Frear wrote about the terror he saw that night. The following paragraphs are taken from his writing.

A tornado of fire

I looked out of one of the south windows. The Courthouse Park was filled with people. The air was filled with falling embers and ash. It looked like a snowstorm lit by colored fire. The glare and the strange light were frightening.

This drawing shows the burning opera house during the Great Chicago Fire of 1871.

My nephew and I ran downstairs. Before beginning our trip, we stopped to get some coffee, which I needed very much. I met several fire fighters, who said that the entire fire department had given up. The men were overworked, and they could do nothing more. While we stood there, a girl was brought in. Her dress had nearly burned from her body.

On the way out, we saw a man unhitching our horse. He jumped into the wagon when we saw him. He would have driven off, but I caught the horse by the head. The man finally sprang out of our wagon, struck my nephew in the face, and then ran east toward State Street. We also headed east.

We drove as fast as we could to Wabash Avenue. The wind swept embers after us. The whole avenue was a scene of terror. People wandered in a daze, and animals darted through the streets. They were being driven mad by the embers that fell and burned them. We could barely guide the horse through the people and other wagons. Looking back west, I saw that State Street was already burning.

Wabash Avenue, the street we were on, also was beginning to burn. The fire was just behind us. Whirling embers beat against the houses and covered the roofs and windowsills. Flames leaped across the street. Sometimes the wind would lift a great body of flames. Then the fire would leap forward like a vicious animal.

Property up for grabs

All the large homes were now being emptied. A mob of men and women, all screaming and shouting, ran about wildly. They bumped into each other as if they had gone mad. We tried to force our way along the avenue, which was already littered with costly goods. But it was not easy.

I finally got out of the wagon to lead the horse. But then I was struck on the arm by a bird cage. Someone had flung it from an upper window. The moment I let go of the horse, he jumped away. He ran into a burning wagon of furniture. The crash threw my nephew out on his shoulder. Luckily, my nephew was not badly hurt. But the horse ran off in terror. I saw him leap like a panther, and then he vanished.

We hurried on toward the St. James Hotel, thinking the girls might be there. On the way, we passed some of the strangest and saddest sights I have ever seen.

Then we reached the stores north of Madison Street. These stores were packed full of goods, and none of them could be saved. People were stopping to load wagons, carts, and even coaches with goods. A vicious crowd of men and boys were joking with each other and tearing open boxes to find out what lay inside.

Using skills and strategies

Self-questioning

Self-questioning means asking yourself questions about something. Asking questions can help you understand things. For example, when you go to new places you might ask, "What street am I on? Is this the place?"

You can also ask yourself questions about what you have read. For example, you might ask yourself why Frear called the men and boys at the store *vicious*. When you go back to the paragraph, you can read that the crowd tore open packages, stole goods, and joked about what they were doing. Frear probably felt that these actions were vicious.

You may ask yourself how Frear felt about the other things he saw. Then find and underline a sentence on the bottom half of page 38 that answers the question.

I reached the St. James between two and three o'clock on Monday morning. Women and children were screaming in every direction. Bags were being thrown about. It was reported that hundreds of people had died in the flames. I now concluded that Mrs. Frear's girls had been lost.

Using skills and strategies

Self-questioning

Why did Frear conclude that his nieces had been lost? The answer is in the paragraph above. Underline the sentence that contains the answer.

Then someone came and said that the bridges were burning; soon there would be no way of escaping to the north or west. Men shouted in panic. Half-dressed women with screaming children fled from the building. I lost sight

This is how Chicago looked after the fire.

of my nephew. Getting out with the crowd, I ran toward
Dearborn Street. The gust of fire behind me was so strong
that I could hardly keep on my feet.

I ran to a hotel, where I found people crammed in the
parlors. Invalids were lying on the floor. Others were
running about. I forced my way upstairs and looked into all
the open rooms, calling out for Mrs. Frear's daughters.

All this time, the top floors were on fire. Soon the smoke
began to roll down the stairways. Most of the people hurried
out of the building. I went up to the fourth story, looking
into every room, kicking open those doors that were locked.
Some other men were searching in the same way.

When I went outside again, it was daylight. The street
was choked with people, who yelled and moaned with
terror. The fire was raging. I had to get over the river. It
would not be easy. The rail of the bridge was broken. How
many people were pushed over the bridge I cannot tell. I
saw one man stumble under a load of clothing and
disappear. The people in the passing boats paid no
attention to him.

Rebuilding a City

Frear did escape the fire. He rejoined his sister-in-law.
They learned that the children had escaped to a safe part of
the city. Many others were not as lucky. About 300 people
died in the fire. Many were invalids who could not escape
on their own. About 90,000 people lost their homes. That
was almost 1 out of every 3 people in Chicago. All together,
about 3½ square miles of the city burned.

In the days after the fire, trains rolled into Chicago. Some
carried food and drinking water; others brought clothes and
tools for rebuilding the city. Within a month after the fire,
there were 4,000 new buildings built in Chicago. The
people of Chicago passed a law that all new buildings must
be made of brick. The spirit of the great city had not died in
the great fire. In fact, the city came back stronger than
ever.

Think About What You've Read

Important ideas

1. How did Mrs. O'Leary's cow cause the Great Chicago
   Fire?

2. How did the wind affect the fire?

_____

_____

Use what you've learned before

3. The people of Chicago were not prepared for a great fire. How was their response different from Amelia Earhart's when her plane crashed?

_____

_____

Important word meanings

Write a sentence for each of the words listed below. Use a separate sheet of paper for your sentences.

terror   embers   vicious   invalid

Using skills and strategies

In the hotel, almost everyone was running downstairs, away from the smoke and fire. Frear, however, ran upstairs. Write a question you might ask yourself about Frear's action. Then write your answer on the lines below.

_____

_____

Writing

Imagine that you are one of Mrs. Frear's children. You were separated from your mother or from your uncle while the fire burned. Write a few paragraphs telling what you saw, did, and felt during that time. Use a separate sheet of paper for your writing.

Your important ideas

Look back over the article. Write down one idea that seems to be the most important one to you—the one idea that you would like to remember.

_____

_____

Your important words

Look back at the words you have learned as you read about the Chicago fire. Write down the word or words you think are most important—those you would most like to remember.

_____

_____

In the Shadow of a Volcano

What do you already know?

Write down three things that you already know about volcanoes. You might write about the causes of volcanoes or the damage they do. Work with a partner, if you like.

1. _____

2. _____

3. _____

Make predictions

Look at the pictures and read the headings in the article. Then write down three things that you think you will learn as you read this article.

1. _____

2. _____

3. _____

Set your purpose for reading

Write down one thing you hope to find out about a volcano as you read this article.

_____

Learn important words

Study the meanings of the words below and the way they are used in sentences. Knowing these words might help you as you read this article.

eruption—the throwing out of lava, steam, or ash from a volcano. *The eruption made a huge black cloud.*

eerie—strange and spooky. *Wandering through the streets of the dead city gave me an eerie feeling.*

archaeologist—a person who studies past human life. *The archaeologist found evidence of a very old city.*

preserve—save from being destroyed or worn down. *The ash from the volcano preserved the city.*

In central Italy, near Naples, there is a volcano called Mount Vesuvius. This volcano towers over the countryside. In the past 200 years, it has erupted 9 times. Each time, it has spouted fire, stone, and ash. The most famous eruption of Mount Vesuvius took place almost 2,000 years ago. It began about noon on August 24 in the year 79 A.D.

An eyewitness report

A young man named Pliny watched the famous event. Later, he described the second day of the eruption. Pliny said the buildings shook as if they would fall apart. Pliny and his mother ran from the town. Crowds of people followed in terror. A horrible black cloud loomed above the land. Sudden bursts of fire flashed. The sea was pushed back from the shore, and hundreds of animals lay stranded on the sand.

Then came the ashes. Pliny wrote that thick smoke rolled in like a flood. Thick, heavy ash covered everything with eerie darkness. People cried, wailed, and shouted. Many believed that the end of the world had come. But then the darkness dissolved, and the sun began to shine. Pliny looked around. The town lay hidden beneath a deep blanket of ashes. It looked like a black snowstorm had buried the earth.

Pompeii lay buried for 1700 years until archaeologists uncovered the city.

Listing things in sequence means listing them in some kind of order. It may be the order in which they happen, from first to last. Or it may be another kind of order—for example, from smallest to largest or youngest to oldest. For example, if you put tools or nails in order, you might order them from smallest to largest.

If you listed the time sequence of some main events in Pliny's story, it might look like this:

1. Buildings began shaking.
2. Ashes began falling.
3. Darkness fell.
4. The darkness cleared.
5. Pliny saw that everything lay buried.

Below you'll read the events leading to the discovery of the buried city of Pompeii. Number the sentences to show the sequence of events by which Pompeii was found.

Three cities were buried by the ash and stone from Vesuvius. People who lived through the eruption left those cities. Through the centuries, the towns were forgotten.

Pompeii is found again

In 1748, workers were building a tunnel near Vesuvius. One worker hit his spade on something buried in the ground. He brought up a block of stone with Latin words on it. Since Latin is a very old language that hasn't been spoken for a long time, the man was excited and curious. He dug farther. He found coins, vases, and weapons. He had discovered the ancient city of Pompeii.

In the years since then, archaeologists have uncovered most of Pompeii. The ash that destroyed Pompeii also preserved much of it. Archaeologists found Pompeii just as it was in the year 79. Buildings still stood in the ash. There was even graffiti, found on walls and doors.

But the most eerie thing about Pompeii is that the remains of the people were preserved there. The ash from Vesuvius buried people where they fell. Over the years, it hardened around them. When their bodies decayed, they left empty spaces in the ash.

Archaeologists poured wet plaster into the air pockets they found. They waited for it to dry. Then they dug away the earth around it. What remained were plaster casts in the shape of the people who had died. The casts showed the exact position in which the person had died. Sometimes they even showed the expression on the person's face.

You just read a sequence telling how archaeologists made plaster casts of the people of Pompeii. Underline the sentences in the article that tell the sequence. Number the sentences to show the sequence for making plaster casts.

Archaeologists found evidence of more than 2,000 victims. Some had fallen as they ran away. Others had stayed in their homes. In one home, 18 people had died clinging to each other. A man held a small girl in his arms.

Looking into the past

Pompeii had been a big city, with tall apartment buildings and large private homes. It had huge public bathhouses and large theaters where musicians and actors performed. Pompeii also had many shops that sold wine, meat, oil, cloth, and baked goods. In fact, this city of 20,000 people had 20 bakeries. In some of them, archaeologists found the remains of baking bread.

The graffiti of Pompeii gives us the strongest sense of a living city. The people of Pompeii had used paint or a sharp nail to write ads or send messages.

A bronze pot is missing from my shop. Anyone who returns it will get a reward.

I won a dice game—and I didn't cheat!

God bless anyone who invites me to dinner.

I am surprised, O Wall, that you have not collapsed with the weight of all the stupid things these idiots have scribbled on you.

The eruption of Vesuvius snuffed out the life of a crowded, noisy city. Yet when it buried Pompeii, it preserved it against the wind and rain that destroyed other ancient cities. The voices of Pompeii speak from the walls and the doorways. The city speaks from beneath the ashes.

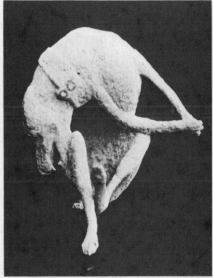
This dog was found in the ruins of Pompeii.

Think About What You've Read

Important ideas

1. What did the eruption of Vesuvius do to Pompeii?

_____

2. What happened to the ash over hundreds of years?

_____

3. How did archaeologists find out what people in Pompeii did when Vesuvius erupted?

_____

_____

45

4. Which person—Frear or Pliny—was in more danger?

_____

_____

Important word meanings

Write the letter of the word on the right next to a related word on the left.

_____ 1. eerie   a. save

_____ 2. eruption   b. odd

_____ 3. terror   c. dig

_____ 4. preserve   d. fire

_____ 5. archaeologist e. fear

Using skills and strategies

The article describes how air pockets were formed where people died in Pompeii. Underline the sentences in the article that describe the sequence of that process. Then number the sentences in the order in which they happened.

Writing

Imagine you were a news reporter back in 79 A.D. when Mount Vesuvius erupted. You were sent to Pompeii to find out what happened.

Write down ideas about the events at Pompeii. Tell how things looked, sounded, tasted, felt, and smelled. Then use your ideas for a news report about Pompeii. Use a separate piece of paper for your writing.

Your important ideas

Look back over the article. Write down one idea that seems to be the most important one to you—the one idea that you would like to remember.

_____

_____

Your important words

Look back at the words you have learned as you read about Pompeii. Write down the word or words that you think are most important—those you would most like to remember.

_____

_____

The Ship That Couldn't Sink

What do you already know?

Write down three things that you already know about ocean liners, icebergs, or the *Titanic*. Work with a partner, if you like.

1. _____

2. _____

3. _____

Make predictions

Look at the pictures and the headings in the article. Then write down three facts that you think you will learn as you read this article.

1. _____

2. _____

3. _____

Set your purpose for reading

Write about something you hope to find out about the *Titanic* as you read this article.

_____

_____

Learn important words

Study the meanings of the words below and the way they are used in sentences. Knowing these words might help you as you read this article.

luxury—beauty and comfort. *The passengers lived in great luxury, with huge rooms and many servants.*

elegant—fancy; showing good taste. *The rich woman always traveled on elegant ocean liners.*

loom—to come into sight; to seem close at hand. *As the fog began to clear, the crew saw an iceberg loom in front of the ship.*

It was the largest passenger ship in the world. From the bottom of the ship to its highest tower, the *Titanic* was as tall as an 11-story building. From end to end, it was as long as 4 city blocks. Its builders said the luxury liner was stronger and safer than any other ship of its kind. They called it "the ship that couldn't sink."

The *Titanic* set sail on its first voyage from England on April 10, 1912. Four nights later, in the middle of the Atlantic Ocean, it struck an iceberg. Within three hours, the elegant ship vanished below the waves. Over 1,500 people went with it to their death.

Life aboard the great ship

On its one and only trip, the *Titanic* carried about 1,300 passengers and 890 crew members. Among its passengers were many first-class passengers. They had paid several thousand dollars each to travel to America in luxury. For them, the ship was like a beautiful hotel. It had elevators and thick carpets. It had pianos and elegant rooms for dancing. It even had indoor swimming pools and a gym.

First-class passengers stayed on the highest levels of the ship. Below them were second- and third-class passengers. These people had paid much less to travel on the *Titanic*. They were not allowed to visit the elegant floors above. They could not use the pools or the gym or the dance floors. And they did not have their own rooms. Still, they were sailing on the best and safest ship on the ocean.

On the night of Sunday, April 14, the ship was just over halfway to New York. The sea was calm, and the clear sky was lit by stars. Just before midnight, two crewmen spotted a huge iceberg looming in front of the ship. Before the ship could change course, it struck the iceberg.

Women and children are loaded into the lifeboats aboard the *Titanic*.

The great ocean liner sinks into the sea.

Emergency!

To this day, no one knows exactly what happened to the *Titanic*. We do know that water began rushing into the lower front rooms. Pumps were switched on. But the pumps couldn't keep up with the flood of water pouring in. Slowly, the ship began to sink. Its front end leaned ever closer to the sea's surface.

Using skills and strategies

Self-questioning

Self-questioning means asking questions about what you read. Doing this helps you think about what you read. It also helps you understand it better. Based on the last two paragraphs, you could ask yourself, "Why didn't the *Titanic* avoid the iceberg?" Then you might answer that the crew members were not careful because they thought the ship couldn't sink. You might answer that the iceberg came into view too late.

You also might ask how the passengers would respond to the danger. Read ahead and underline the sentences that tell how the passengers acted.

Captain E. J. Smith ordered all passengers onto the deck. Many passengers had slept right through the crash. They gathered on deck at the captain's order, but almost no one believed that disaster loomed. After all, the *Titanic* could not sink!

Passengers began boarding the lifeboats. It wasn't easy. The *Titanic* had been at sea for four days, but there had been no lifeboat drills. Few people knew where to go or what to do. Women and children stepped into the lifeboats first. They held tight as the boats swayed and bumped their way to the water. Still, few people sensed the real danger. Many boats were lowered only half full.

Think about how third-class passengers traveled and how the *Titanic* was damaged. Then think of a question about the safety of the passengers in different parts of the ship. For example, do you suppose more third-class passengers died than first-class passengers? Underline any clues you find in the article. Then write a possible answer in the margin.

Then the real tragedy of the *Titanic* became clear. With passengers and crew, there were about 2,200 people on board the great ship. Yet there were lifeboats for only 1,178—even if all the boats were filled. As the front end of the ship sank lower, the passengers crowded to the rear. A few brave ones dived over the side. Some—but not all of them—were picked up by lifeboats. The rest did not survive.

Counting the loss

The ship *Carpathia* was sailing only 58 miles away from the *Titanic* when it got an SOS call. By the time it reached the *Titanic*'s location, there was no sign of the large luxury ship. The crew did find 850 shivering people in lifeboats. And drifting among the boats were icebergs. There were dozens of them. Some of them rose 200 feet above the sea.

Almost all the women and children traveling in first and second class were saved. But those in third class were not as lucky. Half of them died. In fact, more than 1,500 people never saw the *Carpathia*. They had gone to their death with the ship that couldn't sink.

Think About What You've Read

Important ideas

1. List two reasons why the *Titanic* was said to be the best passenger ship of its time.

_____

_____

2. List one difference between traveling on the *Titanic* in first class and traveling in third class.

_____

_____

_____

Use what you've learned before

3. How did the people on the *Titanic* act differently from the people in the Great Chicago Fire?

_____

_____

Important word meanings

All the words below appear in the article. On the lines below, write a sentence for each word. Then erase the word. Trade sentences with a partner. See if your partner can fill in the blanks correctly.

luxury   elegant   looming   preserve

_____

_____

_____

_____

Using skills and strategies

You read that women and children were allowed to board the lifeboats of the *Titanic* before men. Think of some questions about the order in which people were saved. Then write one question in the margin. Discuss your question with a partner.

Writing

Imagine you are an officer around the time the *Titanic* sank. After the disaster, you were asked to suggest changes in passenger ships. List as many ideas as you can. Then write a letter to your boss, stating the changes you would make. Use a separate sheet of paper for your writing.

Your important ideas

Look back over the article. Write down one idea that seems to be the most important one to you—the one idea that you would like to remember.

_____

_____

Your important words

Look back at the words you have learned as you read about the *Titanic*. Write down the word or words that you think are most important—those you would most like to remember.

_____

_____

War of the Worlds

What do you already know?

Write down three things you already know about how people imagine creatures from outer space. Work with a partner, if you like.

1. _____

2. _____

3. _____

Make predictions

Skim the article by reading the first sentence of each paragraph. Also look at the pictures and read the headings. Then write down three things that you think you will learn as you read this article.

1. _____

2. _____

3. _____

Set your purpose for reading

This article is about a false report that Martians were coming. Write down one thing you hope to find out as you read this article.

_____

_____

Learn important words

Study the words below and the way they are used in sentences. Knowing these words might help you as you read this article.

objective—goal or purpose. *The program's objective was to give people a good time.*

desperate—filled with panic; hopeless. *Hundreds of desperate people fled the Martians.*

track—follow. *The announcer said he would track the movements of the Martians.*

incident—event. *Every newspaper reported the awful incident.*

On October 31, 1938, some radio artists put on a scary Halloween play. Their objective was to thrill their listeners. They succeeded. More than six million people tuned in to the radio program. By the time it was over, more than a million listeners were desperately afraid.

Announcer: I guess that's the . . . thing, directly in front of me, half buried in a huge pit. . . . Wait a minute! Someone's crawling out. . . . Someone or . . . something. . . .

The program was called "War of the Worlds." At the beginning, an announcer said that it was only a play. But many listeners tuned in late. They thought they were hearing a real news broadcast. They believed that creatures from Mars were landing in New Jersey. They believed that the creatures wanted to destroy us.

Using skills and strategies

Thinking about what you already know

Thinking about what you already know about a subject helps you understand what you read about that subject. It also helps you know what to expect. For example, when you cook a new dish, you might recall what you already know about the foods you will use to make the dish.

What do you already know about emergency news programs? You probably know they often show many reporters and locations. The reporters may act surprised. They might raise questions that they can't answer. You might expect to learn that the announcers for this radio play did the same things.

For one long hour, the "news broadcasters" tracked the Martians. They gave accounts of Martian machines flying over treetops. They said that people were fleeing the Martian vehicles. They yelled with terror that the Martians were cutting off power lines, railroad tracks, and other means of communication and travel. They guessed that the Martians' objective was to wear us down and take over.

People who tuned in late wondered whether the incidents were real. Some called the police or local radio stations. Some checked the newspaper. They found the program listing for "War of the Worlds." Others figured out that the strange report was science fiction. But many people never guessed the truth. Fear gripped them as they thought about the coming disaster.

Using skills and strategies

Thinking about what you already know

When you read about The Great Chicago Fire, Pompeii, and the *Titanic*, you learned about some of the ways people react to danger. In the margin, write notes about some of the ways people act.

Then write down what you think these frightened listeners might have done. Read ahead and see if this helps you understand what the listeners did.

Orson Welles directed the radio broadcast of the "War of the Worlds." He later became a famous movie director and star.

A picture from the book, *The War Between the Worlds*, shows a Martian leaving a space ship. The radio play was based on the book by H.G. Wells.

Listeners take action

People all over the country started to take action. In New Jersey, farmers grabbed guns. They fanned out to search for Martians. Other people rushed into the streets. They held wet towels to their faces in case poison gas was in the air. Doctors and nurses phoned hospitals. They offered to care for victims of the Martians.

Some people jumped into their cars and raced to join their loved ones. Others sped away without any clear goal. Some people began loading their furniture into cars. Some simply froze in panic.

Then the play's news reporter read a "bulletin." The bulletin said that more Martian vehicles had landed. At first, the Martians were only in New York. Now they were landing in Buffalo, Chicago, and St. Louis. Fear swept over the country.

Hundreds of desperate people phoned police and newspapers about the incident. In Indianapolis, a woman ran into a church. "It's the end of the world!" she cried. "I just heard it on the radio!" Services were dismissed.

One listener told how she panicked when she heard about the Martians: "I kept shivering and shaking. I pulled out suitcases and put them back, started to pack, but didn't know what to take."

A high-school girl in Pennsylvania recalled her own panic. She wondered whether she should stay home or flee. "My two girlfriends and I were crying and holding each other. Everything seemed so unimportant in the face of death. We felt it was terrible we should die so young."

Using skills and strategies

Thinking about what you already know

Think about the times you have played a trick on someone, or someone else has fooled you. Would it work a second time? Why or why not?

Use what you know about being fooled to decide whether the same listeners could be fooled again. Then read ahead to see what some others think.

How could it have happened?

Why did so many believe the story was real? Of course, listeners who tuned in late had missed the statement that it was only a play. After that point, the actors just did a good job of acting like reporters. They made the program seem very real. Three days after the program, a newspaper reporter wrote about the incident. She said it had shown how easy it is to create panic.

Fifty years later, most people laugh about that night of panic. The thought of mean Martians is funny today. But what if the same program were made into a TV special? What if it were shown tonight? Would you keep calm? Or would you track the lights in the sky—just in case?

Think About What You've Read

Important Ideas
1. What did some people think when they tuned in late to "War of the Worlds"?

2. Name two ways in which some people figured out the program was not true.

3. Do you agree that the incident showed how easy it is to create panic? Explain your answer.

Use what you've learned before

4. Did some people in this article act in a helpful way when faced with disaster?

_____

_____

Important word meanings

Fill in each blank below with the correct word.

elegant   desperate   objective   track   incident

1. My _____ is to buy an _____ car.

2. I became _____ when I couldn't lock the door.

3. We filled out a police report on the _____

4. I can _____ the plane with my binoculars.

Using skills and strategies

Imagine that you just tuned into a report that America was being invaded. What would you do to find out if the report was true? Make a list of the things you would do. Explain why you would take these actions, based on what you already know. Use a separate sheet of paper for your writing. Then discuss your answers with a partner.

Writing

Imagine the radio station asked people to write in and say whether they thought the program was a good or a bad idea. Write a letter to the station, telling your opinion. Include your reasons. Use a separate page for your writing.

Your important ideas

Look back over the article. Write down one idea that seemed to be the most important one to you—the one idea that you would like to remember.

_____

_____

Your important words

Look back at the words you have learned as you read about "War of the Worlds." Write down the word or words that you think are most important—those you would like to remember.

_____

_____

Can We End Famine?

What do you already know?

Write down three things that you think you already know about hunger or about ways to feed the hungry. Work with a partner, if you like.

1. _____

2. _____

3. _____

Make predictions

Skim this article and look at the pictures and headings. Then write down three things that you think you will learn as you read this article.

1. _____

2. _____

3. _____

Set your purpose for reading

Think about solutions to hunger you have heard about. Then write about one thing you hope to find out about hunger, drought, or food shortages as you read this article.

_____

_____

Learn important words

Study the meanings of the words below and the way they are used in sentences. Knowing these words might help you as you read this article.

drought—lack of rainfall. *The drought made the plants wilt and die.*

scarce—hard to find; in short supply. *After six months of dry weather, drinking water was very scarce.*

severe—very serious. *The severe lack of water made it hard to grow plants.*

volunteer—person who offers to do something for no pay. *The volunteer brought food supplies to the starving people.*

"**I**'m starving!" If you're like most people, you've probably said that at some time. You might even know how it feels to be almost weak with hunger. But you probably have not gone to bed hungry every night for weeks.

Millions of people in the world really are starving, however. They not only go to bed hungry, they wake up hungry. They live their lives—and die—hungry. They are caught in a disaster called famine. Famine is a shortage of food that lasts a long time and affects a large number of people.

Famine strikes Bihar, India

In 1966, Bihar, India, was in trouble. The area had suffered from a drought for almost two years. Many crops had dried up and died. Most streams were dry, and even drinking water was scarce. Water was so hard to find that wild animals such as tigers and panthers came to the few remaining water holes. That meant the streams in the hills were dry, too. The land looked like a desert.

Using skills and strategies

Taking notes

Taking notes on important ideas can help you remember them. Many people make notes when they have a busy day coming up. They make a list of all the things they need to remember. If you wanted to remember the effects that drought had on Bihar, you might make a list like the one below.

- Crops dried up and died.
- Streams were dry.
- Drinking water was scarce.
- The land looked like a desert.

The people of India have had many famines because of drought, floods, and war.

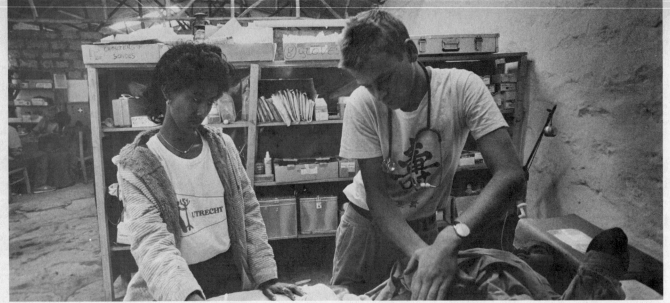

Volunteers prepare food and other goods for areas struck by famine.

Because the crops were dying, food was scarce in Bihar. There was little water, so the people could not raise their own food. They had to buy it. And because there was so little food, they had to pay a high price for it. Soon, prices rose so high that poor people couldn't afford to buy food. Many people became sick, and some of them died.

The severe lack of food and water was most dangerous to babies, children, and old people. The children of Bihar became very thin. They were too weak to run and play. They just sat quietly and stared sadly into space. Though they were hungry, most of them were too weak even to cry. By late 1966, millions of people in Bihar were dying.

Help arrives

Then something else began happening. People around the world heard about the drought. They learned of the danger of famine in Bihar. Ships loaded with food began sailing into Indian ports. Nine million tons of wheat came from the United States. Some of it was sold at low prices in special shops set up by the Indian government. Much of the wheat was given away.

Schools began feeding free meals to the weakest and sickest children. There were five million of them. It took a few months, but slowly the children became healthy again. They gained weight. They had energy to play. Their skin, which had become dull and dry, became brighter.

Another kind of help also came. Volunteers from around the world came to teach farmers new ways of farming. They helped save the few crops that were still alive. With the farmers, they planted new crops that could grow quickly, even in dry weather.

The volunteers also showed people how to dig wells. And then the people of Bihar had a stroke of luck: they found that there was plenty of water under the ground! They built half a million new wells. Soon, Bihar recovered.

60

Using skills and strategies

Taking notes

If you took notes to remember three things that saved Bihar from famine, you might write this.
- Food from other countries
- Help in planting new crops
- Help in finding new supplies of water

Underline the sentences in the paragraphs on page 60 that tell these important facts.

The story of Bihar has a happy ending. The famine was ended before it became a disaster. And the future looked better, too. Thanks to the new wells and new ways of farming, the people of Bihar no longer had to fear dry weather as they had for hundreds of years.

The danger remains

In many other parts of the world, famine—or the fear of famine—remains. In 1983, a severe drought caused a famine in northern Africa. Within a year, one and one-half million people had died. That famine is still going on.

Through the centuries, famine has killed more people than any other disaster. More people have died from famine than from all the hurricanes, tornadoes, earthquakes, volcanoes, floods, and fires put together. More people have died from famine than from all the wars in history.

Farmers try to grow crops in Africa during a severe drought.

The paragraph below tells two ways in which wars cause famine. To remember how war causes famine, take notes on the paragraph.

First, underline the ways in which war causes famine. Then list them in the margin.

In most cases, famine happens because important crops fail to grow. Drought usually kills the crops. But too much rain can also kill them. So can severe storms and plant diseases. Natural disasters can kill plants. So can wars. Wars do not only ruin crops, but they also block roads and keep food from reaching people.

Famine happens most often in poor countries. Even in good times, these countries have very little food. Poor farmers often use very simple, old ways of growing crops. They may not know about new ways to grow more food. Or they may be too poor to buy new tools and machines.

The story of Bihar shows that famine can be ended, even in poor countries. But it won't end by itself. People need to know and care about the danger of famine. Governments must take action. Groups like the United Nations (UN) and the International Red Cross must get more volunteers. We know how to wipe out famine. Now we have to get to work.

Think About What You've Read

Important ideas

1. How does drought help to cause famine?

_____

_____

2. Who suffers the most from famine?

_____

_____

3. Name three causes of famine.

_____

_____

4. Name one way people helped end famine in Bihar.

_____

_____

5. Name one way in which famine is different from other disasters.

Important word meanings

Underline the sentences in the article where these words appear. Then write a sentence of your own for each of the words. Use another sheet of paper for your sentences.

desperate   drought   scarce   severe   volunteer

Using skills and strategies

Pretend that you want to raise money to help fight famine. Use your notes from this article to list three ways in which money can help people facing famine. Write your list on the lines below.

Writing

Imagine that your town has been given a grant. The grant is to be used to help another town anywhere in the world. You want to use the money to help end famine in Africa.

Write notes about the ways in which money and people from your town can help end famine in Africa. Then use your notes to write a short speech telling why the money should be used to end famine.

Your important ideas

Look back over the article. Write down one idea that seems to be the most important one to you—the one idea that you would like to remember.

Your important words

Look back at the words you have learned as you read about famine. Write down the word or words that you think are most important—those you would most like to remember.

Reviewing What You Have Learned

Some facts and ideas you have learned

You have learned many important facts and ideas as you read about disasters. A few of them are listed below. Add your own important ideas to the end of this list. You can look back at the "Your important ideas" section of each lesson to remember the ideas you wrote down.

- During the Great Chicago Fire, some people were kind and helpful, while others were selfish and cruel.
- The graffiti found at Pompeii showed that the people there played games, made jokes, and acted much like we do today.
- The tragedy of the *Titanic* could have been prevented if people had been prepared.
- More than a million people believed "War of the Worlds" was true because it sounded like a real news program.
- We can help end famine by telling people about the problem, helping volunteer groups, and giving money.

_____

_____

_____

Some word meanings you have learned

Here are some of the important words you learned in the articles you read. Make sure you understand their meanings. Then add important words of your own. You can look back at the "Your important words" section of each lesson to remember the words you wrote down.

eerie—strange and spooky. *The fire made the city seem eerie.*

elegant—fancy; showing good taste. *The elegant women wore their pearls on the lifeboats.*

scarce—hard to find; in short supply. *Money is always scarce during a famine.*

_____

_____

Purposes for reading

Look back at the section called "Set your purposes for reading," at the beginning of every lesson. What purposes did you set for reading the articles in this cluster? Were your purposes met? Choose a purpose that was not met by an article you read. Then plan another way to meet your purpose. Use a separate sheet of paper for your writing.

CLUSTER 2

Using skills and strategies

Read the paragraph. Then read the sentences listed below the paragraph. Number the sentences in the sequence that they happened.

When Ted came home from school, he went straight to the freezer. He wanted to eat some of that peppermint ice cream he had bought the night before. But when he opened the freezer, Ted was shocked. The box with the mouth-watering picture was gone. Someone had eaten the ice cream before he'd even tasted it!

_____Somebody ate the ice cream.

_____Ted found that the ice cream was gone.

_____Ted came home from school.

_____Ted bought ice cream.

Writing: persuasion

Imagine that someone is planning to keep children under the age of 17 from watching movies about disasters. Do you think the proposal is a good one or a bad one? Why?

Write a letter to the local paper telling about your views. Explain why you think the way you do. Try to persuade the people in your town to agree with you. Use another sheet of paper for your writing.

Revising

Have a friend read your letter and tell you what he or she thinks. Do you want to change your letter in any way? Do you want to add reasons or make the letter more clear? If so, make those changes.

Activities

1. City life today is different than it was at the time of the Great Chicago Fire. How is the risk of fire different in cities today? Make a list of the ways modern cities are safer from fire. Work with a partner, if you wish.
2. A few years ago, Mount St. Helens erupted in Washington State. Ask your librarian to help you find facts about this eruption. How was it like the eruption that destroyed Pompeii? How was it different?
3. Recently, the *Titanic* was found at the bottom of the Atlantic. Ask your librarian to help you find some reports about the *Titanic* or another famous shipwreck. Report to the class on what has been found.
4. Take notes on an important topic, such as war, pollution, or a natural disaster. Then use your notes to write a newspaper article about the topic. Display your article for the class to read.

Animals

Read and learn about animals

Animals can have a strong effect on people. People keep them as pets, cheer for them in the movies, and wonder at their behavior. Having animals around also makes people feel better.

A 16-year-old boy in California was ill. He lay still, not talking, not moving. Nothing interested him, with one exception—birds. If he saw a picture of a bird, he responded. His eyes followed the picture.

The boy's family took him to a place where animals were trained for movies. He saw the cage holding a trained eagle. The boy wanted to hold the eagle on his arm. The trainer did not object. For the first time in months, the boy spoke and smiled. In the following weeks, the boy came back again and again. Soon he was caring for the eagle. Six months later the boy was fine. The eagle had helped to cure him.

What do you already know about animals?

Talk about what you know. Get together with a group of students to talk about what you already know about animals. Here are some questions to help you get started.
1. What kind of animal would you like to have as a pet?
2. What are some of the ways that animals help us?
3. What rights do animals have?

Write about what you know. Write a few sentences about an animal you have known well.

_____

_____

_____

Make predictions

Read the titles of the articles in this cluster and look at the picture on page 67. Write down three things that you think you will learn about by reading these articles about animals.

1._____

2._____

3._____

Start to learn new word meanings

All the words listed below are used in the two paragraphs on page 66. Study the meanings of these words as you read about animals.

exception—a case to which a general rule does not apply. *Visitors may not touch the animals, but the sick boy was an exception.*

object—to express disapproval or dislike. *Almost everyone objects to cruelty to animals.*

respond—to act in return. *Your dog should respond when you call his name.*

Learn new skills and strategies

One of the strategies you will practice in this cluster is summarizing. Summarizing is useful because it helps you remember the main points of what you have read. You will also learn about reading graphs and framing.

Gather new information

By the end of this cluster, you will have learned the answers to these questions.

1. What makes an animal a good performer?
2. What are some duties of pet ownership?
3. Why isn't it enough just to say that people should be kind to animals?
4. What is the most popular pet in the U.S.?

Animal Stars

What do you already know?

Write down three things you might already know about animals who have starred in movies or television shows. Work with a partner, if you like.

1. _____

2. _____

3. _____

Make predictions

Look at the picture in this article and skim, or look over, the first three paragraphs. Then write three things you think you will learn about as you read the article.

1. _____

2. _____

3. _____

Set your purpose for reading

Write down one thing you hope to find out about animal stars as you read this article.

_____

_____

Learn important words

Study the meanings of the words below and how they are used in sentences. Knowing these words might help you as you read this article.

essential—necessary. *An exciting plot is an essential part of an action movie.*

ham—an actor who tries to steal the show. *The actors were not very interesting, but Tom the cat was a real ham.*

perform—to act; to carry out commands. *My pet hamster can perform three tricks.*

respond—to act in return; to answer. *A well-trained dog will respond to spoken commands.*

Near the end of the movie, the hero dashes into a smoke-filled room. He pulls a woman to safety. She gives him a hug. Then the hero goes off to a reward of dog biscuits.

This scene occurs when the hero is a dog. But dog biscuits are not the star's only reward. Rin Tin Tin performed in the TV series with his name. He lived in air-conditioned comfort and was protected by five guard dogs.

Dogs aren't the only animals that have become stars. Trigger the horse starred with cowboy star Roy Rogers. Mitzi the dolphin was the lead in the movie and TV series *Flipper*. Other stars have included cats, bears, mules, chimps, monkeys, and pigs.

Of course, there have been thousands of other animal performers. But only a few animals have been admitted into the Animal Actors Hall of Fame. Only a few have won the Patsy, the Oscar for animals. What sets the animal stars apart from the animal bit players?

Using skills and strategies

Summarizing

A summary is a short statement of the important ideas in a story or article. When a friend asks what a TV show was about, you don't repeat every word of the program. You tell about the most important happenings and ideas.

Almost every story or article has a beginning, middle, and end. When you summarize, it is often helpful to look for these main parts. So far in this article, you have read the introduction, or beginning. Here is a summary of this part: *Many animals have performed in movies. Only a few animals, however, have become stars. What makes an animal a star?*

As you read the next four paragraphs of this article, watch for the answers to the question in the introduction. You will need these ideas in your summary.

Mitzi the dolphin

Intelligence is essential to animal actors. An animal must learn many tricks and remember them on command.

Fury the horse starred in *Black Beauty* and in his own television series. Fury could limp, kneel, and grin. He could play dead, untie ropes, and obey signals to go left or right. Fury also performed tricks in the right order for each scene.

Mitzi the dolphin could respond to 15 different hand signals and learned new tricks in a matter of hours. She also was a wonderful mimic. She once heard a worker whistling near her tank. She surfaced and whistled back.

The owner and trainer of Rin Tin Tin said that Rinty could respond to more than 500 commands. He could perform such tricks as pulling a bell rope, beating out a fire with a sack, and pretending to attack villains.

Using skills and strategies
Summarizing

The four paragraphs above partly answer the question "What makes an animal a star?" To summarize these paragraphs, you must look for the answer. Underline the sentence above that states the need for intelligence. The rest of the section gives examples of animal intelligence.

As you read the last section, look for a second answer to the question: "What makes an animal a star?" Underline the sentence that states the answer. Then, in the margin, summarize what the rest of the section adds to that idea.

The second essential quality of an animal star is the desire to perform and perform well. The animal must *want* to do what it has learned. It must enjoy pleasing its trainers, fellow actors, and audience. It must be a ham.

The dog Pal was only a double—a stand-in—for the dog who was the star in *Lassie Come Home*. The original star began to shed her coat during filming. The double took her place. One of the big scenes had Lassie swimming across a raging river. Pal obeyed instructions but then improved on the script. When he came out of the river, he pretended to be very, very tired. He walked a few steps and then dropped. According to Hollywood legend, the director of the movie said to Pal's trainer, "Pal went into the river, but Lassie came out."

Trainers and owners of many animal stars have seen this same desire to do a great job in their animals.

Roy Rogers said of his horse, "They threw away the pattern when they made Trigger. During all those hard rides for pictures and television, he never fell once. We had to do more retakes for human actors than for Trigger."

So take a close look at your pet dog or cat or hamster. Is your pet smart? Does it learn new tricks easily? Does it enjoy performing? If you answered *yes* to each question, you may have an animal star in the family.

Think About What You've Read

Important ideas

1. Identify three animal stars discussed in the article.

_____

2. How did a male collie win the role of Lassie?

_____

_____

Use what you've learned before

3. Name a recent movie or TV show in which an animal
   starred. Describe the animal and its role.

_____

_____

Important word meanings

Match each word in dark type with the word that means
the same thing. Write the letter of the matching word.

_____ 1. **essential**   **a.** answer

_____ 2. **ham**   **b.** show-off

_____ 3. **perform**   **c.** necessary

_____ 4. **respond**   **d.** act

Using skills and strategies

On a sheet of paper, write a short summary of this article.
Use what you wrote in the margins to help you.

Writing

Imagine that you have acted in a movie with a dog or
horse star. On a sheet of paper, describe the experience.

Your important ideas

Look back over the article. Write down one idea that
seems to be the most important one to you.

_____

Your important words

Look back at the words you have learned as you read
about animal stars. Write down the word or words that you
think are most important.

Owning a Pet

What do you already know?

Write down three things you might already know about owning a pet. Work with a partner, if you like.

1. _____

2. _____

3. _____

Make predictions

Look at the pictures in this article. Read their captions, or explanations. Then write down two things you think you will learn about as you read this article.

1. _____

2. _____

Set your purpose for reading

Write down one thing you hope to find out about owning a pet as you read this article.

_____

_____

Learn important words

Study the meanings of the words below and how they are used in sentences. Knowing these words might help you as you read this article.

breed—a group of animals with the same ancestors and the same qualities. *Terriers are a breed of small dogs.*

custodian—a person responsible for the care of a building. *Ask the custodian to fix the leaky pipe in the kitchen.*

object—to express disapproval or dislike. *Many people object to keeping large animals as pets in apartments.*

responsibility—a thing or person that one must care for. *The mice in the science lab are the responsibility of the science class.*

Dear Uncle Bob,

Remember that letter I wrote last month? I'll guess I sounded pretty much like a loser. I know I was feeling sorry for myself. The idea of Mom and Dad's divorce was bad enough. Moving to a new apartment and starting a new school just made things worse. Thanks for the funny get-well card you sent. It made me start to think.

The same day your card came, I saw a television program about a special kind of medicine—pets. On the program, doctors and other people said that pets are good for you. Some hospitals let dogs and cats visit the children's wards, and some kids get well faster because of the pets. And there are nursing homes that have pets. Many old people feel better when they have a cat or dog to talk to or hug.

Well, I figured that if I was sick, I should take some medicine. And a pet sounded like great medicine. If I had a pet, maybe I wouldn't notice that I don't have any friends in the neighborhood yet. And besides, having a pet might give me a way to meet people. I could just imagine myself taking a great big Siberian husky down the street for a walk. Everyone would stop to look and talk.

Using skills and strategies

Problem-solution

When you face a problem, you figure out a way to solve it. You make a plan. Then you follow your plan until you solve the problem or face a new one.

Many articles follow this same pattern. The writer states a problem. Then he or she discusses a way to solve the problem. Sometimes the steps lead to a quick solution. Other times the steps lead to other problems.

In this article, the speaker's main problem is loneliness. His solution is buying a pet.

As you read the following paragraphs, find out whether the solution will be easy or will cause other problems.

Most children, sick or well, respond to an animal.

If you live in the country, a sheep might be a good pet.

Clearly, getting a pet was a very smart idea. But Mom doesn't always understand my smart ideas. So I decided to test out my suggestion on someone else first. You probably guessed I usually don't go to my little sister for help. This time I was forced to. My talk with Andrea went something like this:

Me: What do you think of our getting a pet?
Andrea: Wow, what a great idea!
Me: I was thinking about a Siberian husky.
Andrea: Wow, what a dumb idea! I'd guess there are rules in the apartment building against dogs and cats.
Me: So why did you say getting a pet was a great idea?
Andrea: Well, I was thinking about a pet we could keep in a tank or a cage, like a goldfish or a mouse.

But who ever took a goldfish or a mouse out for a walk? I decided my next step would be to discover the apartment-building rules.

Using skills and strategies

Problem-solution

The paragraphs above brought up two problems with the writer's idea. Underline the problem the writer may have with his mother. Then underline the sentence that states the problem that Andrea raised. Keep reading to see how the writer solved his problems.

The custodian said that small pets were allowed, as long as they were quiet and you cleaned up after them. If the neighbors complained about barking or other noises, you had to get rid of your pet. I asked what he meant by *small*. After all, a husky is smaller than a pony. He didn't think I was very funny. So I guessed that a husky was out.

At that point I went to the library. I read half a dozen books about dogs. I learned about the different breeds, how to take care of a dog, and how to train it. I began to realize that getting a dog wasn't a short-term thing, like being the new kid on the block. Once I had a dog, he or she would be my responsibility—and my friend—for 10 or 20 years. I liked that idea—a friend for years and years.

The more I read, the more I wanted a dog. I couldn't understand why I had waited so long. My only problem was trying to choose the kind of dog that was best for me. Each breed had good points.

Using skills and strategies

Problem-solution

One problem was solved when the writer learned that the apartment owners allowed dogs. He still has two problems to solve before he can overcome his main problem. The main problem is the writer's desire for a dog to cure his loneliness. His other two problems are:

1. Will his mother let him have a dog?
2. What kind of dog should he get?

As you read the rest of the article, look for the solutions to the two problems. Write the solutions to the problems in the margin.

Last week I talked with my mom. I told her that I wanted a dog, and that Andrea didn't object. I said I'd feed my dog and train it. I'd brush it and clean up after it. I'd take it to the vet for shots and checkups. I'd take it for walks every day to keep it healthy.

I must have said the right things. When I finished, all Mom said was, "Just remember, the dog will be *your* responsibility. The family can afford the dog. But all the daily care will be yours. Now, what kind do you want?"

I shrugged. "I don't know. I just need a dog."

"Well, then," she said, "let's find a dog that needs you."

The next day Mom and I went to the city animal shelter. The people there let me walk between rows of cages that held dogs nobody wanted. In a way, I felt awful. I knew that dogs left at a shelter for too long are killed. I wanted to take *all* of them home. But I knew I wouldn't be able to take care of them, and they'd be back in a few days. So I looked for just the right dog for me.

Finally I saw her. She was a little terrier who bounced up and down in her cage as I came near. She needed room to play in and someone to play with. She needed me.

So, Uncle Bob, there's a new member of the family. Doc and I take walks, or runs, around the block every day. When can you come to visit us and meet her?

Your nephew,
Joe

Think About What You've Read

Important ideas

1. Why does Joe want a pet? How will a pet help?

_____

_____

2. Why do you think Joe's mother didn't object to a dog?

_____

_____

Use what you've learned before

3. If Joe wants Doc to become an animal performer, what must he do?

_____

Important word meanings

The following eight words were used in the two articles you have read. Use as many of the words as you can in two sentences. Write on a separate sheet of paper.

breed	custodian	essential	ham
object	perform	respond	responsibility

Using skills and strategies

Think of a problem you have had that involves an animal—a pet, a neighbor's pet, or a wild animal. On a separate paper, explain your problem and the solution you found.

Writing

Write a paragraph about a pet you want. Tell the steps you would take to choose that pet. Write on a separate sheet of paper.

Your important ideas

Look back over the article. Write down one idea that seems to be the most important one to you—the one idea that you would like to remember.

Your important words

Look back at the words you have learned as you read about the question of owning a pet. Write down the word or words that you think are most important—that you would like to remember.

Animal Rights

What do you already know?
Write down three things that you think you already know about rights of animals. Work with a partner, if you like.

1._____

2._____

3._____

Make predictions
Skim this article briefly. That is, look it over for easy-to-notice ideas and for words that are used several times. Then write down three things you think you will learn about as you read this article.

1._____

2._____

3._____

Set your purpose for reading
Write down one thing that you hope to find out about animal rights as you read this article.

_____

_____

Learn important words
Study the meanings of the words below and how they are used in sentences. Knowing these words might help you as you read this article.

advocate—a person who speaks in support of something. *The workers at the cat shelter are advocates of animal rights.*

interfere—to get in the way. *If you see a child treating a pet badly, you should interfere.*

society—an organized group of people with a common interest. *Turtle owners may join the Turtle Society.*

zebra—an African animal that looks like a striped horse. *The zebra is a fast runner.*

On the plains of Africa, a zebra roams its area, looking for food. It faces dangers every day. A dry spell could leave it with little to eat. A lion could attack it. But the zebra can go where it likes and be with its own kind.

In a zoo in America, a zebra paces in its area, closed in by fences. It is fed and watered every day. It is safe from enemies. It is given the best of care. But it is not free to roam or to choose its mate.

Even though this zebra is well cared for, some people feel sorry for it. These people believe that humans have no right to lock the zebra in a zoo. They believe that the zoo interferes with the rights of the zebra.

Using skills and strategies

Framing

Imagine that you're at a football game. When the two teams line up, you know that the ball is between them. You also know that the play will start when the center snaps the ball to the quarterback. Then the quarterback will hand the ball to a runner, throw the ball, or run with the ball. Because you know these things, the game is easy to watch. Your knowledge of how the game is played is a *frame* that helps you follow the action.

The same thing applies to reading. You must keep in mind the writer's *frame*—the way the information is organized. Then you can use that frame to help you follow the ideas that the writer is presenting.

In the beginning of the article, the writer compares and contrasts two things—zebras in Africa and zebras in the zoo. If you recognize that frame, you are able to understand more of what you read.

Sometimes a writer explains a thing by listing its parts. The following section uses that frame. As you read, look for the five rights of animals. Underline each right.

The animal-rights movement wants to change the way people treat animals. Animal-rights advocates say that animals have rights and humans should respect them.

Animal-rights advocates agree that animals should have these rights:

1. The right to enjoy their life according to their basic nature. For example, if they enjoy exercise, we may not keep them penned up.
2. The right to good health. Pets and farm animals deserve decent food and care.
3. The right to be comfortable and to avoid pain.
4. The right to a painless death. If we must kill an animal for food, we must make that death as easy as possible.
5. The right of their kind to live. We may not destroy all wildlife areas just to make room for ourselves.

Zebras graze on the African plain.

Using skills and strategies

Framing

Sometimes writers use a frame that tells what happens first, second, third, and so on. This frame is called sequence. As you read the next section, decide which frame is being used. Then circle the correct term.

comparing and contrasting   sequence

The animal-rights movement is not new. Throughout history, most people treated their animals well. Many religions taught that kindness to animals is a good habit. But many people still were thoughtless or cruel. Advocates of animal rights finally decided that laws were needed to stop the cruelty.

In 1641, the leaders of the Massachusetts Bay Colony passed a law to protect animals. This was the first animal-rights law in North America. In 1826, New York passed the first *state* law to protect animals. The law applied only to animals owned by people, not to strays. Sad to say, the law was not strong enough to protect many animals.

In 1865, Henry Bergh saw many horses treated badly in New York City. The wealthy man would try to stop cart and carriage drivers who were beating their horses. He knew, however, that he could not stop the problem by himself. So in 1866 he founded the American Society for the Prevention of Cruelty to Animals, the ASPCA. Many people joined the society. Together they worked to improve conditions for working animals, pets, and strays.

After that, other groups across the United States founded anticruelty societies. Today many of those societies are still active in the struggle for animal rights.

Using skills and strategies

Framing

You know that writers sometimes state a problem and then discuss how to solve the problem. This kind of frame is called problem and solution. As you read the last section, decide how the ideas are developed. Which of these two frames do you find? Read and decide. Then circle the correct term.

problem and solution   **time order**

Not all animal-rights advocates agree on what animals deserve. For example, some advocates say that people should not eat meat. Other advocates point out that many animals are themselves meat eaters. They say that people may eat meat as long as the animal is killed painlessly.

Another big disagreement concerns using animals to test new drugs. Some animal-rights advocates say that all testing should stop immediately. Others point out that testing on animals has led to cures for many diseases. They say that to stop animal testing will cause human deaths.

What do you think? Do we need more laws to protect animals? Or will more laws only interfere with the work of farmers, zookeepers, and others who deal with animals?

Before you make up your mind, learn more about these questions. Contact your local ASPCA and library for information. Read what different animal-rights advocates have to say. Find out what people who disagree with the animal-rights movement say. Then you can decide where you stand on animal rights.

Think About What You've Read

Important ideas
1. What major thing did Henry Bergh do for animals?

_____

2. Some people say that a zoo interferes with the rights of animals in the zoo. To which of the five animal rights do they refer?

_____

3. Why do many animal-rights advocates not eat meat?

_____

Use what you've learned before
4. Do you think that owning a pet interferes with the rights of animals? Give a reason for your opinion.

_____

_____

_____

Important word meanings
Use each word in the list once to complete the paragraph.

advocate   essential   interfere
responsibility   society   zebras

The members of the _____ worry that bad weather and hunters

will kill all the _____ in Africa. They believe they have a

_____ to _____ with this disaster. Their

spokesperson, or _____, says that zoos are _____

aids for keeping this kind of animal alive.

Using skills and strategies
The frame called cause and effect tells what events cause other things to happen. The frame called question and answer asks a question and then discusses the answer. Review the article titled "Animal Stars." Decide which of these frames is used. Circle the correct term.

cause and effect   question and answer

Writing
Decide whether you support zoos or object to them. List at least two reasons for your opinion. On a separate sheet of paper, write a paragraph to convince your best friend that your opinion is the right one to have.

Your important ideas
Look back over the article. Write down one idea that seems to be the most important one to you.

_____

_____

Your important words
Look back at the words you have learned as you read about animal rights. Write down the word or words that you think are most important.

_____

_____

Selecting a Pet

What do you already know?

Think about the kinds of pets that you, your friends, or other people own. Write down three things you know about pets. Work with a partner, if you like.

1. _____

2. _____

3. _____

Make predictions

Look at the graphs in this article. Read their titles and labels. Then write down three things you think you will learn about as you read the article.

1. _____

2. _____

3. _____

Set your purpose for reading

Write down one thing you hope to find out about pets as you read this article.

_____

_____

Learn important words

Study the meanings of the words below and how they are used in sentences. Knowing these words might help you as you read this article.

exception—a case to which a general rule does not apply; a person or thing different from the others in that group. *Frogs usually are not friendly, but my frog is an exception.*

license—a paper or tag showing that permission has been granted, for example, permission for animal ownership. *Almost every city requires a license to own a dog.*

Almost everyone loves some kind of animal. Some people are happy just to hear bird songs or to visit a zoo now and then. Others enjoy reading about a favorite animal. Hundreds of millions of people around the world share their homes with pets.

Nobody knows how many pets there are, even in our own country. Some pets, such as dogs, must have licenses. That gives us a good idea of their number. But many others don't need licenses. These pets, such as cats, have never been counted exactly.

It's difficult even to decide which types of animals to count as pets. Everyone thinks of dogs and cats, of course. But these are certainly not the only pets. A pet store may have 30 or 40 kinds of animals. In addition to animals that live in people's homes, pets such as horses live in stables and barns. There are also very unusual pets, such as pet monkeys.

Using skills and strategies

Using pictorial aids

When you watch a movie, you learn through your eyes as well as through your ears. Pictures often tell more than words. In books, too, pictorial aids can give much information. These aids include photographs, drawings, maps, graphs, and tables. They add details to the main ideas in the text.

For example, the third paragraph on this page states that there are many kinds of pets. What pets are shown in the picture below? List their names in the margin.

Before you adopt a pet, you must be aware of many facts. Perhaps the most important fact is that adopting a pet means taking on a long-term responsibility. Just how long your responsibility lasts depends on the type of animal you choose.

As a rule, smaller animals have shorter lives than larger animals. Some people think this is because a small animal wears out its body more quickly. Its heart beats faster than a large animal's heart. The small animal breathes more often and uses up energy more quickly. Mice, for example, rarely live more than two years.

Two exceptions to the rule are cats and dogs. Even though cats are usually smaller than dogs, cats live longer. A healthy dog often lives into its teens. Many cats live past 20 years old.

The graph below shows the greatest age recorded for several animals. Remember, this is the greatest age. The average animal of each kind does not live as long as the record-setters listed here.

Using skills and strategies

Using pictorial aids

Examine the bar graph on this page. Under each name below, write the age of the oldest animal of that kind at its death.

dog   cat   Shetland pony   parrot   box turtle

The Oldest of Their Kinds

Box turtle	(129 years)
Cat	(31 years)
Catfish	(60 years)
Chimpanzee	(47 years)
Dog	(29 years)
Elephant	(77 years)
Fin whale	(43 years)
Hummingbird	(8 years)
King vulture	(40 years)
Lion	(30 years)
Mouse	(2 years)
Pigeon	(30 years)
Shetland pony	(48 years)

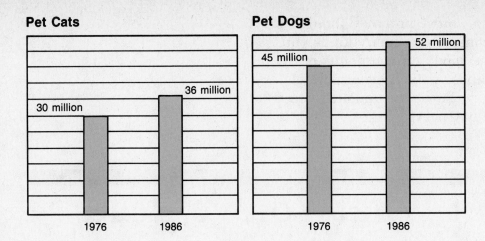

Pet Cats

30 million — 1976
36 million — 1986

Pet Dogs

45 million — 1976
52 million — 1986

As a pet owner, you may decide to stick with the favorites—dogs and cats. The number of dogs and cats in the U.S. is always growing. The graphs above give estimates—that is, reasonable guesses—for the number of pet cats. The number of pet dogs is based on the number of dog licenses issued. The numbers do not include stray cats and dogs.

Using skills and strategies

Using pictorial aids

Use the bar graphs above to answer these questions.
1. *In 1986, were there more cats or dogs in the U.S.?*
2. *How many more dogs were in the U.S. in 1986 than in 1976?*

Use the pie charts below to answer this question.
3. *What percent of farm households have both cats and dogs?*

Write your answers in the margin.

Many families can't decide between cats and dogs. So they have at least one of each. For many years, many farms have had both cats and dogs. In recent years, even city families have found room for both pets in one home.

Percent of Households with Both Cats and Dogs

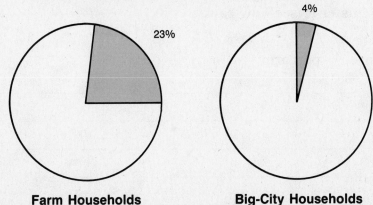

23% — Farm Households

4% — Big-City Households

Even if you don't own a pet, you've probably thought of getting one. Before you do, consider the many kinds you can choose from. Find out the good and bad points of each. Keep in mind the responsibilities you will be accepting. Then decide. If you choose a pet, usual or unusual, you will join millions of people who enjoy pets.

Think About What You've Read

Important ideas
1. Name three pets other than cats and dogs.

_____

_____

2. Why is it easy to find out how many dogs are pets in the U.S.?

_____

3. Do you think that this article should tell the reader which kind of pet is best? Why or why not?

_____

_____

_____

Use what you've learned before
4. How would you select a pet if you wanted it to become a star?

_____

_____

Important word meanings
Write sentences about the animals in the picture on page 83. Use one of the words below in each sentence. If you like, look back at the articles in this cluster to see how each word is used.

       breed   exception   license   perform

_____

_____

_____

_____

Using skills and strategies

Examine this graph showing the speeds of several fast animals. Find the fastest animal on land. Circle its name in the first column of the chart. Do the same for the fastest animal in water and the fastest animal in the air.

Speeds of Animals in Miles per Hour

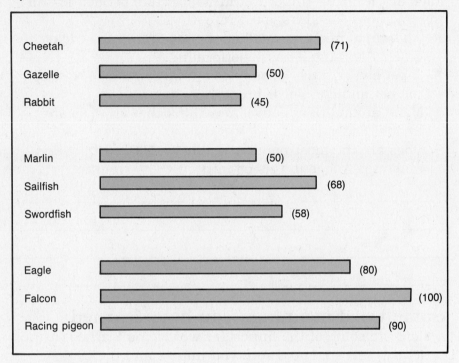

Cheetah	(71)
Gazelle	(50)
Rabbit	(45)
Marlin	(50)
Sailfish	(68)
Swordfish	(58)
Eagle	(80)
Falcon	(100)
Racing pigeon	(90)

Writing

Write about an unusual pet—other than a cat or dog—that you would like to have. Tell what it looks like, how it acts, and what makes it special. Use a separate sheet of paper.

Your important ideas

Look back over the article. Write down one idea that seems to be the most important one to you—the one idea that you would like to remember.

_____

_____

Your important words

Look back at the words you have learned as you read about pets. Write down the word or words that you think are most important—that you would like to remember.

_____

_____

Reviewing What You Have Learned

CLUSTER 3

Some facts and ideas you have learned

You learned many important facts and ideas as you read about animals. A few of them are listed below. Add your own important ideas to the end of this list. You can look back at the "Your important ideas" section of each lesson to remember the ideas you wrote down.

- An animal must be intelligent enough to learn tricks quickly and must enjoy performing.
- A pet owner must be sure he or she can afford to keep the pet and care for it properly.
- Many animal-rights advocates think that animals are treated badly.
- Dogs are the most popular pet in the U.S., with over 52 million pet dogs in this country.

_____

_____

_____

_____

Some word meanings you have learned

Here are some of the important words you learned in the articles you read. Make sure you understand their meanings. Then add important words of your own. You can look back over the "Your important words" section of each lesson to remember the words you wrote down.

advocate—a person who speaks in support of something. _Advocates of zoos point out how well they help people learn about animals._

essential—necessary. _An essential part of training an animal is to be firm with your commands._

responsibility—a thing or person that one must care for. _A pet is its owner's responsibility._

_____

_____

_____

Purposes for reading

Look back at the section at the beginning of every lesson called "Set your purpose for reading." Is there a purpose you did not meet? Tell where you might find information to help you achieve this purpose.

_____

_____

Using skills and strategies

Read the paragraph below. Identify its frame—how the information is organized. Circle one of these frames:

time order   **cause and effect**   **problem and solution**

At this moment, thousands of stray cats and dogs are roaming about every big city. They are hungry, often sick, and sometimes dangerous. Where do they come from? Too often, they come from unwanted litters. People whose pets have litters often have no way to care for the new kittens and puppies. They take the animals to a strange place and dump them. The best way to solve this problem is to stop the pets from having litters. A small, almost painless operation will save a cat or dog from producing future strays.

Writing: persuasion

Write a letter to a film director. Explain why your pet should be the star of his or her next movie. Point out the special qualities and abilities that make your pet a natural for the movies. If you don't have a pet, make one up. Use a separate sheet of paper.

Revising

Trade papers with a partner and read your partner's paper as if you are the movie director. Do you think your partner's pet deserves a starring role? If so, tell your partner what made you feel that way. Choose the strongest reasons listed in the letter. If not, explain why your partner's reasons are weak. When you get your paper back, make any changes that are needed.

Activities

1. With a small group of classmates, prepare a debate on animal rights. First choose a topic, such as "Testing on animals is necessary and should be continued." Next do research on the topic. Then divide your group into two teams, for and against the statement. Have your debate in front of the class.
2. The Broadway musical *Cats* featured actors made up to look like cats. With a group of friends, check at the library for information about the musical and how the actors were made up. Then with your teacher's help, make yourselves up to look like cats or other animals. Wear your disguises in class for a day. Try to move as much like animals as possible. Write a report about your experiences.
3. Write a story in which your pet is the hero. Read it to the class.
4. Take photographs of neighborhood pets. Put together a display or folder of your photos.

Explorers

Read and learn about explorers

Since the beginning of time people have been curious about the world around them. They have explored new ideas and traveled to all parts of the globe. Their work has resulted in discoveries that form the basis of our way of life.

In this cluster, you'll read about an explorer who studied the world of microbes. His work, done centuries ago, still saves lives today. You'll also read about explorers like Christopher Columbus who discovered the New World. Some explorers, like Columbus, hoped to find riches or a new route across the ocean. Others tried to expand knowledge about a particular subject that would benefit everyone. Their work is not done. The world always needs more explorers.

What do you already know about explorers?

Talk about what you know. Get together with a group of students to talk about what you already know about explorers. Here are some questions to help you get started.
1. Who are some famous explorers you know about?
2. What did they discover?
3. What are some discoveries that need to be made today?

Write about what you know. Name an explorer you have read about or seen in movies. What did this person explore? What did this person hope to discover?

_____

_____

_____

Make predictions

Read the titles of the articles in this cluster and look at the picture on page 91. Write down three things that you think you'll learn by reading these articles about explorers.

1. _____

2. _____

3. _____

Start to learn new word meanings

All of the words below are used in the two paragraphs at the top of page 90. Study the meanings of these words as you read about explorers.

microbe—a living thing that is too small to be seen without a microscope. *The study of microbes has helped scientists cure some diseases.*

route—way to go; path. *The old spice route from Europe to Asia was long and costly.*

expand—to make larger. *The scientist tried to expand our knowledge of the planets.*

Learn new skills and strategies

One of the skills and strategies you will learn about in this cluster is *visualizing*. When you visualize something, you create a picture in your mind. This helps you remember the things you read about. You will also learn about semantic mapping and evaluating what you read.

Gather new information

By the end of this cluster, you will have learned the answers to these questions.

1. Why did people try to find an ocean route through North America?
2. How was the world of microbes discovered?
3. Did very many people become rich during the California Gold Rush of 1849?
4. What is the biggest problem underwater explorers faced in the past?

Search for the Northwest Passage

What do you already know?

Write down three things that you already know about early explorers in North America. Work with a partner, if you like.

1. _____

2. _____

3. _____

Make predictions

Look at the map and read the headings in the article. Then write down two things you think you will learn as you read this article.

1. _____

2. _____

Set your purpose for reading

Write down one thing you hope to find out about how explorers found and crossed the Northwest Passage as you read this article.

_____

_____

Learn important words

Study the meanings of the words below and how they are used in sentences. Knowing these words might help you as you read this article.

passage—a road, path, or course through which something passes. *Magellan discovered a passage for his ships between the Atlantic and Pacific oceans.*

abandon—to withdraw from something in the face of danger. *They had to abandon their ship after it was caught in the ice.*

route—way to go; path. *The old spice route from Europe to Asia was long and costly.*

You may not know us. We are the ghosts of explorers past. For 500 years, we risked our lives searching for the Northwest Passage. Some of us froze to death. A few drowned. Others disappeared and were never heard of again. I'll tell you how it happened.

Spices, treasure of Asia

You don't worry about spices today because you have refrigerators. In Europe long ago, spices kept our food from spoiling. If some food spoiled anyway, we used spices to keep it from tasting bad.

In Europe, we got spices from Asia. We traveled east to get them. The trip was long and costly. In 1492, Christopher Columbus claimed he could reach Asia faster by traveling west. The king and queen of Spain sent Columbus and a few of us to find a western route to Asia. Instead of reaching Asia, we landed in the Americas. We did not find a quicker way to reach Asia.

The Strait of Magellan

Next Ferdinand Magellan and a different group of us sailed from Spain to search for a shorter way from the Atlantic Ocean to the Pacific. Magellan discovered a southern passage in 1520. This narrow seaway near the southern tip of South America allowed ships to sail from the Atlantic to the Pacific. Today you call this passage the Strait of Magellan.

We weren't happy with the southern passage to Asia, however. The trip through the Strait of Magellan took as long as the old eastern route to Asia. We needed a passage through North America—a Northwest Passage. This would be the shortest route between Europe and Asia.

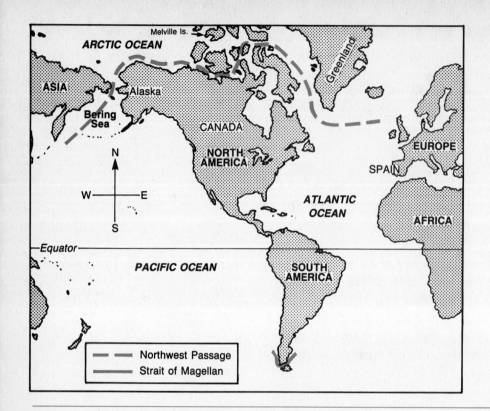

Using skills and strategies

Visualizing

When you read, picture in your mind, or visualize, what you are reading. This helps you understand important ideas. For example, to understand the two paragraphs above, you need to visualize the voyage of Ferdinand Magellan.

Look at the map on this page. Draw a line from Spain through the Strait of Magellan and then northwest to the equator. You can see the route from Europe through the Strait of Magellan and on to Asia was very long. Now imagine how sailors with Magellan felt as they traveled through unknown waters for months and months.

Other European explorers dreamed of discovering a Northwest Passage. Among us are the ghosts of Sir Francis Drake, Captain James Cook, and many others who tried to find the passage but failed. Yet we never gave up.

The cold, cold North

For centuries our ships explored the waters around Alaska, Greenland, and northern Canada. We sailed for 1,000 miles through Canada's Arctic islands. We dodged icebergs 300 feet tall in the Atlantic. Imagine ice as high as a 30-story building. It approaches your ship, closer and closer! The cold wind tosses you around. You drift, never sure when the next iceberg might appear and crack your ship open. We sailed until our ships could go no farther. Then we traveled across the land. If we lived to tell the story, someone else learned from our adventure.

In 1845, the icy waters swallowed 129 of us. Robert McClure and his crew searched for the lost explorers. After our ship, the *Investigator*, was frozen in the ice for 3 winters, we abandoned it. McClure led the crew east over the ice to Melville Island. There a rescue ship picked us up, but the new rescue ship also had to be abandoned later. We spent 2 more winters locked in the ice until we finally broke through and continued on foot. It took us almost 8 years, but Robert McClure's crew traveled from the Pacific to the Atlantic along a Northwest Passage in 1854.

Using skills and strategies

Visualizing

Trace a route on the map on page 94 that could be the route McClure followed. Begin in the Bering Sea. Continue overland to Melville Island. Sail east by ship to the Atlantic Ocean. Label your route *Northwest Passage*. Imagine traveling through this passage for 8 years.

The future

In the 1900s, other explorers made the entire trip by sea. Today only a few ships travel through the Northwest Passage. The voyage is still hard. The United States would like to transport oil by ship through the Northwest Passage. It would save money. The use of icebreakers and other modern equipment may make this possible.

We, the ghosts of all the explorers, can only pass on our knowledge. New explorers need to find a way to open the Northwest Passage for all the countries of the world.

Think About What You've Read

Important ideas

1. Why did the king of Spain send Columbus west to find Asia?

_____

_____

2. Describe the kind of people who became explorers.

_____

_____

3. If you were traveling by ship from Europe to Asia today, what route would you take? Explain your reasons for choosing that route.

_____

_____

Use what you've learned before

4. Why were the explorers afraid of icebergs?

_____

_____

Important word meanings

Write *same* next to the pairs of words that mean almost the same thing. Write *opposite* next to the pairs of words that have opposite meanings.

1. **route** path _____

2. **passage** crossing _____

3. **abandon** remain _____

Using skills and strategies

On the lines below, describe how McClure and his crew probably must have felt when they finally reached the Atlantic Ocean. Write your answer so that a reader can imagine the men's feelings.

_____

_____

_____

Writing

Imagine you are on a ship traveling through the Northwest Passage. On a sheet of paper, write an entry for your diary. Tell what year it is and why you are making this journey. Describe what you are doing and how you feel.

Your important ideas

Look back over the article. Write down one idea that seems to be the most important one to you—the one idea that you would like to remember.

_____

_____

Your important words

Look back at the words you have learned as you read about the Northwest Passage. Write down the words that you think are most important—that you would like to remember.

_____

_____

Exploring with a Microscope

What do you already know?

Write down three things you already know about microscopes and what they do. Work with a partner, if you like.

1. _____

2. _____

3. _____

Make predictions

Look at the pictures and read the headings in the article. Then write down three facts that you think you will learn as you read this article.

1. _____

2. _____

3. _____

Set your purpose for reading

Write down one thing you hope to find out about exploring with a microscope as you read this article.

_____

_____

Learn important words

Study the meanings of the words below and how they are used in sentences. Knowing these words might help you as you read this article.

microbe—a living thing that is too small to be seen without using a microscope. *The study of microbes has helped scientists cure some diseases.*

magnify—to make larger in size; to enlarge. *Scientists use a microscope to magnify very small things.*

lens—a piece of glass or other material, curved in a special way to make objects appear larger or smaller. *A microscope can have one lens or a few lenses.*

The human eye sees many things. Certainly it can see a leaf, an ant, or a grain of sand. A microbe, however, is too small for the eye to see. The mysteries of some microbes have taken hundreds of years to explore.

No one knew microbes existed until about 300 years ago. At that time, people first began using lenses made of glass. The lenses were put into microscopes. A microscope magnifies things so much that very small objects can be seen. With microscopes, a whole new world opened up. Scientists saw things they had never seen before. They started to look more closely at the world around them.

Using skills and strategies

*Evaluating what
you have read*

In school you are sometimes asked to write a report about a certain topic. When you find an article on your topic, you have to evaluate the article, or decide whether it has the information you need.

Imagine you are asked to write a report about Robert McClure's search for the Northwest Passage. You find the article "Search for the Northwest Passage." To evaluate it, you would skim the article first. By skimming it, you'd find out that only one paragraph is about Robert McClure. You'd need more information than that for a report.

Now imagine that you will write a biography on Antonie van Leeuwenhoek that includes his childhood, his goals, and his career. As you read "Exploring with a Microscope," decide whether it gives you enough material to do this. Put an *X* next to any paragraph that contains information you could use in a biography of Leeuwenhoek.

Antonie van Leeuwenhoek

In the late 1600s, a Dutch scientist, Antonie van Leeuwenhoek, spent much of his time grinding glass lenses and making microscopes. He made a dozen, then a

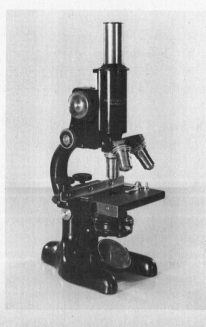

A microscope made in 1665 (left)
and a modern microscope (right)

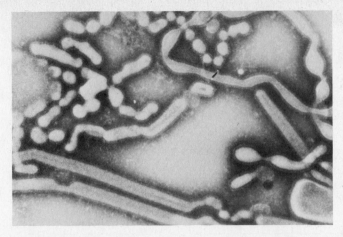
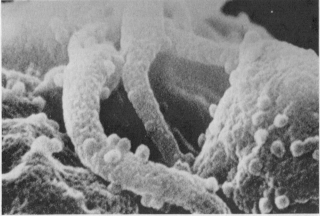

The pictures show the microbes that cause flu (left) and AIDS (right).

hundred. Each one magnified objects better than the one before. For most of his life, Leeuwenhoek put things that interested him under a microscope. Because he lived for 90 years, he had plenty of time to experiment with his microscopes.

Leeuwenhoek started by looking at ox eyes and the hairs of sheep. He looked at the brain of a fly and at the scales of his own skin. Then he put a drop of water under one of his microscopes, and another, and another! Leeuwenhoek's experiments never stopped.

Leeuwenhoek saw what he called "little animals." They were a thousand times smaller than anything seen with the naked eye. They swam around, jumped, and darted from place to place. Leeuwenhoek was excited. He collected hundreds of water samples and examined each one.

Good and bad microbes

Leeuwenhoek observed microbes eating a dead fish taken from a canal. This explained how the waterways of Holland stayed clean. He realized that dead matter was quickly eaten up by the tiny creatures. Leeuwenhoek discovered many different microbes. Then he sorted the small creatures into good and bad microbes. Leeuwenhoek said that the bad ones caused many diseases.

Leeuwenhoek's explorations led to cures for many diseases. In the last 300 years, scientists have made better microscopes. They've used them to discover microbes that were too small to be seen with Leeuwenhoek's lenses. Some scientists have learned how to destroy many bad microbes, or germs. Others have invented ways to grow good microbes that can destroy bad microbes.

Using skills and strategies

Evaluating what you have read

As you read "Exploring with a Microscope," did you find enough information to write a biography about the life of Antonie van Leeuwenhoek? Write your evaluation in the margin. Give reasons for your answer.

Think About What You've Read

Important ideas

1. Why were microbes unknown more than 300 years ago?

_____

_____

2. Why did Leeuwenhoek divide microbes into good and bad ones?

_____

_____

Use what you've learned before

3. Which explorers have helped people more—the ones who explored microbes or the ones who explored the Northwest Passage? Explain your answer.

_____

_____

Important word meanings

On a sheet of paper, answer the questions below.
1. How does a **lens magnify** something?
2. What would you expect to see if you looked at a **microbe** under a microscope?
3. Why did some explorers **abandon** their ships in the Northwest **Passage**?

Using skills and strategies

If you were asked to write a paragraph about an explorer, could you use the information in this article? Why or why not? Write your answer on a separate sheet of paper.

Writing

Imagine that Leeuwenhoek suddenly appears in modern-day America. Of course he wants to study something with his microscope. He doesn't know what today's diseases are, so he asks you for advice. On a separate paper, write down what things you might advise him to study.

Your important ideas

Look back over the article. Write down one idea that seems to be the most important one to you.

Your important words

Look back at the words you learned as you read this article. Write down the words you think are most important.

Prospecting for Gold

What do you already know?
Write down three things that you think you already know about searching for gold. Work with a partner, if you like.

1. _____
2. _____
3. _____

Make predictions
Read the headings and look at the map and pictures. Then write down three things you think you will learn as you read this article.

1. _____
2. _____
3. _____

Set your purpose for reading
Write down one thing you hope to find out about the search for gold as you read this article.

_____

_____

Learn important words
Study the meanings of the words below and how they are used in sentences. Knowing these words might help you as you read this article.

glint—gleam; flash. *The bright glint of the gold helps people to find it when it is lying on the surface of the soil.*

prospector—one who searches for minerals or metals such as gold, silver, and copper. *The discovery of gold in California encouraged many people to become prospectors.*

expand—make or grow larger. *The United States, which began as thirteen colonies on the East Coast, has expanded to many times its original size.*

Shortly after Columbus discovered America, explorers from Spain conquered Mexico and Peru. They found advanced Indian cultures. They also found large amounts of gold. Because the Spanish were greedy for the gold, they killed many Indians and destroyed their cities. Some of the Spaniards traveled to southwestern parts of what is now the United States. They looked for gold but found none and left.

California becomes part of the United States

In the mid-1800s, the United States was a smaller country than it is today. Much of the Southwest, including California, was part of Mexico. The United States wanted to expand onto this land. The two countries went to war. In 1848, the United States defeated Mexico and gained what is now the southwestern part of the U.S.

Since the 1500s, few people had searched for gold in California. There were no prospectors and no miners, until an unexpected discovery was made.

Using skills and strategies

Semantic mapping

Think of a word—such as *gold*—and see what other words come to mind. You may say *shiny, metal, yellow*. Now think of ideas about gold. You may ask yourself what gold looks like, where it is found, why people want it, and so on. You can write related words or ideas in a chart. This is called semantic mapping.

A semantic map for *gold* has been started below. Fill in the spaces. When you are finished, compare your semantic map with those of your classmates.

Gold

What it looks like	Where it is found	Why people want it

The discovery

One morning in 1848, James Marshall, a carpenter from New Jersey, was watching over the digging of a sawmill in California's Sacramento Valley. In order to operate, a sawmill needs a stream or a river. So the plans for building the mill called for deepening the nearby riverbed.

That morning the bright sun began to strike small shiny objects in the riverbed. James Marshall noticed the glint of metal. He suspected that the flakes were gold, but he had to

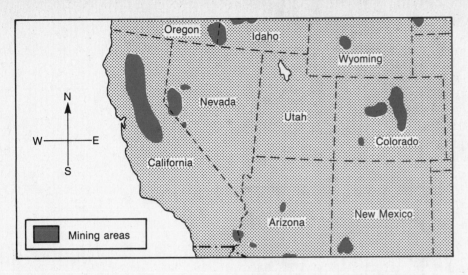

prove it. Marshall went to John Sutter, the man who had hired him. Together they tested the tiny bits of metal. The flakes were indeed gold. With his watchful eye, Marshall had discovered a deposit of gold that stretched 150 miles along the foothills of the Sierra Nevada Mountains.

Forty-niners

The discovery was kept secret for a few months, but soon the news spread across the country. The whole nation caught "gold fever." Thousands of gold seekers headed for California. They were called "forty-niners" because the year was 1849.

The journey from the East was long and difficult. Many forty-niners died along the way. About 40,000 people reached California by sea. Some of them sailed through the Strait of Magellan. Others sailed only as far as Panama. Then they risked disease by hiking across Panama to the Pacific Ocean. From there they sailed north to California.

This prospector hunted for gold in California and Colorado for 65 years.

Forty-niners pan for gold in California.

The strongest explorers took the 2,000-mile overland route, across the American desert and the Rocky Mountains. Some 6,000 wagons, carrying about 40,000 people, moved west in one year over the California trail.

Using skills and strategies

Semantic mapping

In your semantic map about *gold*, you were able to use words that describe gold and tell how it is used. Some words, however, bring to mind a variety of ideas. For example, the word *valuable* may make you think of things that are valuable, such as money or knowledge. You can show this by listing the word's synonyms—words with almost the same meaning—and antonyms—words with opposite meanings.

Below, a semantic map for *valuable* has been started. Fill in the lines with any words or ideas that would help someone understand what *valuable* means. When you are finished, share your ideas with your classmates.

Valuable

What it describes	Synonyms	Antonyms
a treasure	rare	worthless
money	expensive	common

In the margin, write a sentence using three of the six words you used to complete this semantic map.

Panning and mining for gold

Once in California, most prospectors looked for surface gold on the ground or in riverbeds. A washing pan or a box was all they needed to gather it. First they threw a handful of dirt from a riverbed into the pan. Then they poured water over the dirt and rocked the pan. As the dirt washed away, the heavier gold stayed at the bottom. If prospectors found a large amount of gold by panning, they dug deeper near the river and in the hills. The work was hard, prices were high, and living conditions were poor.

Nearly 2 billion dollars in wealth was taken from the earth before the gold became too difficult to find. Nevertheless, few prospectors struck it rich. After a few years, the gold fever faded.

While they were in California, the forty-niners built camps and towns that grew rapidly and were abandoned once the gold was gone. Some prospectors who didn't strike gold became farmers in California and in neighboring states. However, the attention the West Coast received during the gold rush was a big reason people came to northern California and San Francisco later to settle the land.

Think About What You've Read

Important ideas

1. In the 1500s, why did Spain conquer Mexico and Peru?

2. Why did the U.S. go to war with Mexico in the 1800s?

3. If you had lived during the time of the California gold rush, do you think you would have been a "forty-niner"? Why or why not?

Use what you've learned before

4. If you had gone to California in 1849, how would you have traveled there from the East Coast? Tell why you chose the route you did.

Important word meanings

On a sheet of paper, make a crossword puzzle. Use the words *glint, prospector, expand, abandoned*, and *route*. First attach the words to each other for the puzzle.

When all the words are in your puzzle, get a clean sheet of paper and draw boxes to take the place of the letters. Number each box that will begin a word.

Write the headings *Across* and *Down* and make up a meaning clue for each word. Number your clues to match the numbers in the boxes. Give your puzzle to a friend to complete.

Using skills and strategies

You have used semantic mapping to tell about words. Now you can create your own semantic map. Think about how you can explain what a prospector is to somebody who has never heard the word before. Maybe you can name synonyms for *prospector*, tell what prospectors do, tell what tools prospectors need, and so on.

Write *Prospector* in the center of a sheet of paper. Draw a map like the ones on pages 102 and 104. Write a heading at the top of each column. You can use the ideas mentioned above for headings. Then list words or ideas under each heading. When you are finished, compare your semantic map with those created by your classmates.

Writing

Imagine you're a film writer writing the script for a movie about the California gold rush. Plan the characters in your movie. On a separate sheet of paper, write a short description of the movie's three main characters. Explain who they are and what kind of roles they will play in the story.

Your important ideas

Look back over the article. Write down one idea that seems to be the most important one to you—the one idea that you would like to remember.

Your important words

Look back at the words you have learned as you read about prospecting for gold. Write down the words that you think are most important—that you would like to remember.

The Aquanaut

What do you already know?

Write down three things you already know about exploring the ocean. Work with a partner, if you like.

1. _____

2. _____

3. _____

Make predictions

Look at the pictures and read the headings in "The Aquanaut." Then write down three things you think you'll learn as you read.

1. _____

2. _____

3. _____

Set your purpose for reading

Write down one thing you hope to find out about the world under the ocean as you read "The Aquanaut."

_____

_____

Learn important words

Study the meaning of the words below and how they are used in sentences. Knowing these words might help you as you read this article.

aquanaut—an underwater explorer. *The aquanaut spent the whole day exploring the ocean.*

grouper—a large tropical fish that swims near the bottom of the ocean. *The crew of the* Calypso *named the friendly grouper Ulysses.*

chamber—any enclosed space or compartment. *The diving chamber had room for three aquanauts to live underwater.*

I found myself inside a metal chamber large enough for two or three people. In the center was a narrow, winding stairway leading to a door at the top. At eye level, there were many windows. Through one, I could see brightly colored fish. I moved around the chamber looking through each window. There was coral in the shape of a fan outside the first one I looked through. A dark outline outside another might have been a shark. A school of tuna swam lazily past a different window. The largest fish I'd ever seen, a swordfish, approached the last window. I was somewhere in the ocean. It didn't matter how I'd gotten there—it was fantastic! I'd always dreamed of becoming an aquanaut.

For a long time, I looked out on a world I couldn't touch. A huge grouper, the same color as its surroundings, put its face against the window. It blinked and kept its body still as if it were watching me. Looking out the window at the grouper, I realized that the chamber was rising. I was too excited to be afraid.

Using skills and strategies

Evaluating what you have read

You often need to make judgments, or evaluate what you read. For example, imagine that you are looking for information about life in the ocean as part of a homework assignment for your science class. You must decide if an article has good science information. As you read "The Aquanaut," decide whether it presents material you could use for a science report about life in the ocean. Put an *X* next to every paragraph that has information you could use.

A diver waves hello to a friendly grouper.

People who explore the ocean must carry the oxygen they need with them.

On board the *Calypso*

Soon the chamber stopped rising. I saw the glint of sunlight on the water's surface.

The latch above me opened. "How did you like Ulysses?" asked a man with a French accent. "Ulysses is the grouper you were watching. Welcome to our ship, the *Calypso*. I'm Jacques Cousteau," the man continued.

Stepping outside the chamber I met a slender, white-haired man. We shook hands. "Would you like to explore the ocean with an Aqua-Lung next?" Cousteau asked. Then he told me about the Aqua-Lung he'd helped to invent.

The Aqua-Lung

Cousteau explained that exploring the ocean had always been difficult because the divers couldn't breathe underwater. To solve the problem, he and Emile Gagnan invented scuba-diving equipment that is as good as a lung. *Aqua* means water. Their lung for use in the water was called an Aqua-Lung. It allows divers to breathe underwater using compressed air from tanks on their back.

Captain Cousteau showed me the diving equipment on the *Calypso*. The crew helped me put on the oxygen tanks, goggles, and breathing tube I would need underwater. They explained how to use the equipment. I learned quickly that exploring the ocean was a serious matter. I listened to all their instructions and followed each one carefully. Two experienced divers went into the water with me.

A silent, beautiful world

We dove 100 feet below the surface. The silence amazed me. A school of fish made room for us as we swam past. There were barracudas with sharp teeth and brightly patterned eels, but for some reason we weren't frightened.

We swam along with a grouper bigger than Ulysses. Then I hitched a ride on the back of a giant sea turtle. Sea animals that looked like flowers shrank in size as we passed them. As we went away they grew back to their normal size.

Like a roller coaster, a swift, warm current carried us through a narrow channel. Thousands of fish of all colors, shapes, and sizes rode the underwater river with us. Even a blue shark glided past. Swimming against the current, the shark scooped up little fish that were driven into its mouth by the current.

We saw much more than I can say here. When I finally awoke, I was dizzy from my all-night adventure.

Using skills and strategies

Evaluating what you have read

Now decide whether or not "The Aquanaut" is information about the ocean that could help you with your science homework. In the margin, evaluate the use of "The Aquanaut" for this purpose.

Think About What You've Read

Important ideas

1. Describe the world found by the underwater explorer.

_____

_____

_____

2. Explain how you think the aquanaut's diving equipment works.

_____

_____

_____

3. The author of this selection gave it a surprise ending. Tell what the surprise is. Then evaluate the use of the ending. Did it make the selection more interesting for you? Why or why not?

_____

_____

_____

Use what you've learned before

4. Would you rather explore life in the ocean today or have searched for the Northwest Passage in the past? Explain your answer.

_____

_____

_____

Important word meanings

On a separate sheet of paper, write a short paragraph. Use all five of these words in your paragraph: _grouper, aquanaut, chamber, expand_, and _glint_. Look back at the way the words are used in "The Aquanaut" to be sure you use them correctly.

Using skills and strategies

If you were looking for an article to read for extra credit in your history class, which selection in this cluster would be the best one? Evaluate the selections. Write down the article you chose and tell why you chose it.

_____

_____

_____

Writing

The narrator of "The Aquanaut" had always dreamed of exploring the ocean. If you could do any kind of work you wished, anywhere in the world, what job would you choose? Write a paragraph that tells what your work would be like and why you chose it. Use a separate sheet of paper.

Your important ideas

Look back over the article. Write down one idea that seems to be the most important one to you—the one idea that you would like to remember.

_____

_____

_____

Your important words

Look back at the words you have learned as you read about the aquanaut. Write down the words that you think are most important—that you would like to remember.

_____

_____

_____

Reviewing What You Have Learned

Some facts and ideas you have learned

You learned many important facts and ideas as you read about explorers. A few of them are listed below. Write your own list of important ideas. You can look back at the "Your important ideas" section of each lesson to remember what you wrote down.

- A short route was needed from Europe to Asia. People hoped to find a Northwest Passage through North America that would be shorter than going around South America.
- In the late 1600s, Antonie Leeuwenhoek experimented with microscopes and discovered the world of microbes.
- Eighty thousand people went to California to prospect for gold. Two billion dollars' worth of gold was discovered. Few prospectors struck it rich.
- In the past, divers couldn't explore the ocean because they couldn't breathe underwater.

_____

_____

_____

_____

_____

_____

Some word meanings you have learned

Here some of the important words you learned in the articles you read. Make sure you understand their meanings. Then add important words of your own. You can look back at the "Your important words" section of each lesson to remember the words you wrote down.

magnify—to make larger in size; to enlarge. _In order to read the directions for her Aqua-Lung, the diver used a special glass to magnify the words._

glint—gleam; flash. _The bright glint of gold helps people find it when it is lying on the surface of the soil._

aquanaut—an underwater explorer. _The aquanaut spent the whole day exploring the ocean._

_____

_____

_____

_____

Purposes for reading

Look back at the section at the beginning of every lesson called "Set your purpose for reading." Did your purposes help you discover information? Write down one purpose and tell how it helped you in your reading.

Using skills and strategies

Read the first page of "The Aquanaut" again. Then, visualize what you think the chamber and the ocean look like. On a sheet of paper, draw the chamber and everything that is near it. Label the things in your drawing. Think of more than just what is seen through the windows.

Writing: persuasion

Imagine that you are an explorer with many years of experience. You are writing in the journal you keep when you are exploring.

On a separate piece of paper, explain what you are exploring. Then describe something there that frightened your crew. Tell how you convinced them not to turn back.

Revising

Look over the journal entry you have written. Make sure that you said where you are, what frightened your crew, and how you convinced them not to turn back.

Activities

1. Talk to a science teacher in your school. Arrange to see a microscope and learn how to use it. Ask if you can study a drop of water under the microscope. Then draw what you see.
2. If possible, visit an aquarium in your town or city. Choose at least one thing there that interests you. Study it by reading books about it or by talking with aquarium personnel about it. Report to the class what you learned.
3. Try to visualize what a prospector's pan or box looked like. Then with a partner or a few other people try to build one.
4. Read part or all of a Jacques Cousteau book about his underwater adventures. Two good books by Cousteau are *The Living Sea* and *The Silent World*.
5. Find a list of discoveries by explorers in a book such as *The World Almanac and Book of Facts.* Choose one that interests you and read about it in a book on that subject. Tell the class what you learned.

Media

Read and learn about media

The runner has just broken the world record for the 200-meter run. A TV reporter talks to her for the evening news. The reporter asks her about her record time and gets the facts about how she feels. They discuss the Summer Olympic Games. This information is broadcast into homes all over the country.

TV, radio, newspapers, books, and movies are called "mass media" because they communicate with large numbers of people. Mass communication is possible because of the technology of radio waves and modern printing. People can see, hear, and read about events all over the world almost instantly.

What do you already know about media?

Talk about what you know. Get together with a group of students to talk about what you already know about media. Here are some questions to help you get started.

1. How does a reporter get information?
2. What are some ways to send information over long distances?
3. What media do you use?

Write about what you know. Which medium—radio, TV, movies, books, or newspapers—do you think is most important? Why? Write your opinion on the lines below.

_____

_____

_____

Make predictions

Read the titles of the articles in this cluster and look at the picture on page 115. Write down three things that you think you'll learn by reading these articles about media.

1. _____

2. _____

3. _____

Start to learn new word meanings

All of the words listed below are used in the two paragraphs at the top of page 114. Study the meanings of these words as you read about media.

technology—the use of knowledge to reach a goal. *Technology helped them make the huge shark that you saw in* Jaws.

broadcast—to send out by radio or television. *The radio station broadcast the story about the flood.*

communication—giving or trading information by speaking or writing. *Communication between sea and land is important for the captain of a ship.*

Learn new skills and strategies

One of the skills you will learn about in this cluster is taking notes. You can take notes to help you remember facts and ideas for a test. You can take notes when you find information you want to use in your writing. You will also learn about framing and clarifying.

Gather new information

By the end of this cluster, you will have learned the answers to these questions.
1. How does a news story get to the newspaper?
2. How has the way books are made changed since the first books were made?
3. Why are some movies so popular?
4. Who invented the radio?
5. What is the fastest way to send a letter?

Sports Reporter

What do you already know?

Write down three things that you already know about sports reporters and how they do their work. Work with a partner, if you like.

1. _____

2. _____

3. _____

Make predictions

Look at the pictures in this article. Read the first sentence of each paragraph. Then write down three things that you think you will learn as you read this article.

1. _____

2. _____

3. _____

Set your purpose for reading

Write down one thing you hope to find out about sports reporters as you read this article.

_____

_____

Learn important words

Study the meanings of the words below and how they are used in sentences. Knowing these words might help you as you read this article.

journalism—the work of writing or editing a newspaper, book, or magazine. *She's studying journalism because she wants to be a reporter.*

editor—a person who corrects mistakes and checks facts in another person's writing. *Newspaper editors must make sure all the facts in a story are correct.*

interview—a meeting in which two people talk over something. *I asked for an interview with the new pitcher.*

deadline—the latest possible time to do something. *The editor hurried to finish his work before the deadline.*

What part of the newspaper do you read first? Many people start with the sports section. They want to read about their favorite baseball and football teams. They find stories about players, coaches, managers, and owners. They can read about high-school and college sports, too. The sports section also finds room to tell about other sports such as tennis, golf, horse racing, boxing, and track.

Have you ever wondered where all this information comes from? Newspapers get sports news from two sources. Their reporters cover the events. Other sports news comes from news services, such as the Associated Press (AP) or United Press International (UPI). They send information directly to the newspaper offices. The information may be printed exactly as it is received, or reporters can use it in their own stories.

Using skills and strategies

Taking notes

You take notes of important ideas to help you remember what you read. Your notes should only include important information. Your notes should be short and be written in your own words. A good time to take notes is after you have read one or two paragraphs. Here are some notes on the first two paragraphs. *Many people read sports first. News comes from reporters and wire services.*

As you read the next paragraphs, take notes for each paragraph. Write them in the margins. Remember to be brief. Write just enough to remind you about the information in the paragraph.

A reporter and an editor discuss a story in the newsroom.

A newspaper writer checks the story she wrote using her computer.

Jack Stuart is a sports reporter for a Chicago newspaper. Jack studied journalism in college. Then he went to work for the newspaper. He used to work on the picture desk. But he loved to talk about sports, and he always wanted to write about them. When he heard about an opening for a sports reporter, he applied and got the job. Jack's job allows him to use both his interest in sports and his training in journalism.

Jack's working day begins at 7:00 A.M. He goes to a meeting of the sports staff. The sports editor assigns the writing jobs to the reporters. She asks Jack to write an article about the All-Star game. His deadline will be on Friday. Today he's going to cover the Cubs game.

After the meeting, Jack checks the news services. He reads the sports news that has come in. He finds some information that he might use in his article on the All-Star game. He takes notes. Then he's off to Wrigley Field with his portable computer over his shoulder.

Jack arrives at the ballpark early—about 11 o'clock. He wants to have an interview with the coach before the game. He puts his computer aside and takes out his notebook. The coach tells him about the Cub's new pitcher. Jack asks some questions, and he takes notes about the pitcher. He wishes the coach good luck and goes to the press box to watch the game.

The game starts. Jack takes notes on his computer. Between innings, he writes about his interview with the coach. After the game, he'll put all his notes together for his article.

Using skills and strategies

Taking notes

The rest of this article tells how Jack gets his story in the paper the next day. As you read, take notes about the process of getting a story in the newspaper. Write your notes in the margin.

The game ends at 3:30. Jack has two hours until his 5:30 deadline. He writes his story and reads it over a few times. He connects his computer to a telephone in the press box. The story is sent to the computer at the sports desk at the paper.

While Jack waits in the press box, the sports editor looks at his story. She decides how much space to give it on the front page of the sports section. Then she sends it to the copy editor's computer. The copy editor checks it for correct spelling and grammar. He tries to fit the story into the space. It's three lines too long. He calls Jack in the press box, and they decide how to cut the story. Now Jack's part in the news story is over.

At the paper, the night crew takes over. Another editor sends Jack's story to the composing room. It's set in type. The printing presses will roll through the night. Cubs fans will read all about the game early the next morning.

Think About What You've Read

Important ideas

1. How does Jack get his story about the Cubs game to the editor at the newspaper?

---

2. What does the copy editor do to Jack's story?

---

3. Why do you think Jack keeps track of information from the wire services?

Use what you've learned before

4. What important news stories have you already read about in this book?

_____

_____

_____

Important word meanings

You may have used these words in the notes you took: _journalism, editor, interview, deadline._ On a sheet of paper, use each word in a sentence about Jack's job.

Using skills and strategies

Read the following paragraph. On the lines below, write some notes that would help you remember this information.

Feature articles provide extra information about a sports event or a person in sports. A feature article might tell about the history of a sport. It might tell how someone got started in a sport and how that person trains to keep his or her skills sharp. Feature articles sometimes appear in special magazine sections in Sunday papers.

_____

_____

_____

_____

Writing

Think about your favorite sports star. On a sheet of paper, write a paragraph that might appear in a news story about that sports star.

Your important ideas

Look back over the article. Write down one idea that seems to be the most important one to you—the one idea that you would like to remember.

_____

_____

Your important words

Look back at the words you have learned as you read about sports reporting. Write down the word or words that you think are most important—that you would like to remember.

_____

_____

How a Book Is Made

What do you already know?
Write down three things that you already know about how a book is made. Work with a partner, if you like.

1. _____

2. _____

3. _____

Make predictions
Look at the pictures and headings in the article. Then write down two things that you think you will learn as you read this article.

1. _____

2. _____

Set your purpose for reading
Write down one thing you hope to find out about how a book is made as you read this article.

_____

_____

Learn important words
Study the meanings of the words below and how they are used in sentences. Knowing these words might help you as you read this article.

invention—something that is made or thought of for the first time. *The printing press was an important invention.*

scroll—a roll of paper or material like paper with writing on it. *A long time ago people rolled a book into a scroll.*

bind—to fasten sheets of paper together with a cover to make a book. *Huge machines collect and bind the pages between covers.*

cylinder—a long, round object with flat ends, often a part of a machine. *A printing press has several cylinders. Some spread the ink and some carry the paper.*

A light bulb over a cartoon character's head means that he or she has an idea. Books are like those light bulbs. Every book starts out as someone's bright idea.

But books must be printed on paper to become more than an idea. Printed books are one of our most useful inventions. They let us store information, carry it around, and find it when we need it.

Using skills and strategies

Framing

Imagine what would happen if people wrote articles in this way: First, they put all their ideas on little pieces of paper. Next, they threw all the pieces of paper into a jar. Then, they mixed up the papers. Finally, they took each idea out of the jar and wrote it down in the order it was picked.

Of course, writers don't work this way. They take their ideas and organize them carefully. Writers have a framework, or a frame, for their ideas. If you understand the frame a writer uses, you can understand more of what you read.

The paragraphs that follow compare and contrast how books were made a long time ago. Comparing and contrasting is the writer's frame.

Write the answer to this question as you read the next section: *What was the difference between the books people made in 2700 B.C. and the books people made in 700 A.D.?*

This book was made in the 1400s using a printing press.

Books made by hand

The first books were printed by hand. In 2700 B.C., people in Egypt wrote on papyrus. This material was made from the woody stems of the papyrus plant. (Our word *paper* comes from the word *papyrus*.) They used ink made from berries, tree bark, and ashes. Then they rolled up the papyrus to make a scroll.

About 3,400 years later, in 700 A.D., books looked more like our books. People still made them by hand, but they didn't roll the paper into scrolls. They cut it into sheets. Then they folded the sheets and sewed them together along the folds.

The books had covers, too. This meant that you could open the books and read from the middle. If you wanted to read from the middle of a scroll, you had to unwind half the book. Then you had to rewind it when you were finished.

In 700 A.D., every page in every book was written by hand. Each picture was drawn by an artist. The people who wrote most of the books were called scribes. They made copies of the Bible. They copied ancient Greek and Roman writings. They wrote new books about everyday life. Scribes had no deadlines. They always had plenty of time to do their work.

Every book was a work of art. Many people wanted to own books. But making them by hand took a long time. What invention helped people make more books in a shorter time? If you said the printing press, you're right!

The printing press

The first printing presses were made more than 500 years ago. Each letter of the alphabet was on a separate piece of metal. To set up a page, the printer put the letters for the words in a box. Then he put ink on the letters and pressed a piece of paper on the box. He could print many copies of a page. One of the first books printed in this way was a Bible. About 200 copies were made. Today, more than 500 years later, there are 21 copies of this book left.

Using skills and strategies

Framing

The rest of the article tells about modern methods of making books. The author uses the frame of sequence. As you read, write three steps in the bookmaking process in the margin. List the steps in the sequence, or time order, that they occur.

How books are made today

Modern printing methods make books very quickly. Computers set up to 30,000 letters in a minute. Presses print one-half million pages in an hour. Thousands of covers are put on books in a day.

Printers use computers and cameras to set the words in books today. First, the words are put into a computer. Next, the words are arranged on the computer screen the way they will appear on the page. Then, a camera takes a picture of the words, and the picture is developed on a piece of film.

But books are not all type. There are photos and drawings, too. Special cameras make film for all the drawings and photos for a book. Then the film with the words and the film with the pictures are taped together into pages. The new film of the finished page is used to make a plate for the printing press.

Printing plates are made of thin metal or metal and plastic. They're so large that many pages can be put on one plate. In that way, many pages can be printed at the same time. The plates are fitted to huge cylinders on printing presses.

Ink wets the plates on the cylinders. Paper moves under the cylinders, and the pictures and the words are printed on the paper. Some presses can print both sides of the paper at the same time. Some presses can print more than one color at a time.

The pages come off printing presses in huge sheets. A machine folds and trims the sheets. Folding them in the right way puts the pages on each sheet in the right order.

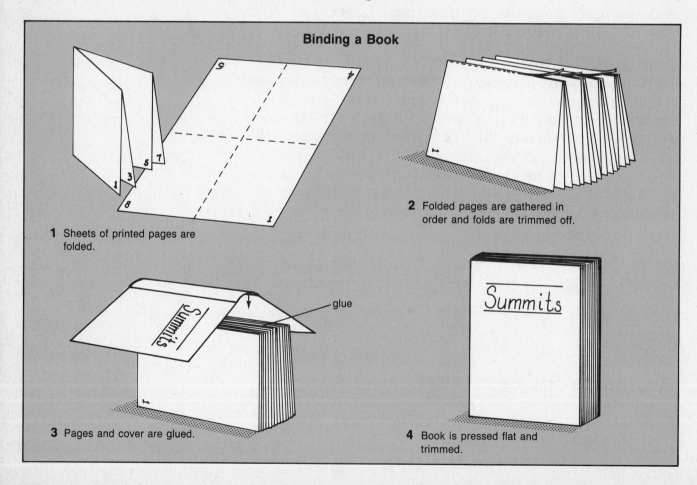

Binding a Book

1 Sheets of printed pages are folded.

2 Folded pages are gathered in order and folds are trimmed off.

3 Pages and cover are glued.

glue

Summits

4 Book is pressed flat and trimmed.

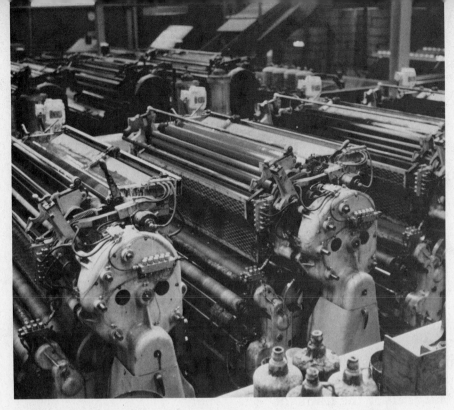

A modern printing press can print 500,000 pages per hour.

Binding machines put the sheets together to make a book. First, the sheets are collected and put in the right order. Next, they are sewn or stapled together. Then, they are pressed flat and trimmed.

The last step in making a book is putting the cover on. A soft cover, like the one on this book, is printed on heavy paper. It is folded and glued on the sheets by machines. The finished books are stacked and put in boxes. Then they are delivered to schools and stores to be used and enjoyed by people like you.

Think About What You've Read

Important ideas

1. How were the first books made?

_____

_____

2. Why are books made around 700 A.D. considered works of art today?

_____

3. Why do you think people save books that were made a long time ago?

_____

_____

4. How is the way that books are bound different from the way newspapers are put together?

_____

_____

Important word meanings

On a sheet of paper, make up a sentence for each of these words: *invention, scroll, bind, deadline.* Instead of writing the words in the sentences, write them at the bottom of the paper. Leave a space in each sentence where the word belongs. Check each sentence to be sure that only one word makes sense in each sentence. Give your paper to a classmate and see if he or she can fill in the correct words.

Using skills and strategies

An author using the problem and solution frame will state a problem and then talk about possible solutions. Suppose the author of "How a Book Is Made" used the frame of problem and solution to organize the article. Circle the question you think the article would have answered.

1. How do printers put the words for a book into their computers?

2. What kind of paper is best for printing books?

3. What difficulties must be overcome to make books more quickly?

Writing

On another sheet of paper, write a paragraph telling all the ways you use books. Do you use them to find information you need? Do you use them for entertainment? Be specific in your paragraph.

Your important ideas

Look back over the article. Write down one idea that seems to be the most important one to you—the one idea that you would like to remember.

_____

_____

Your important words

Look back at the words you have learned as you read about how books are made. Write down the word or words that you think are most important—that you would like to remember.

_____

_____

The Ten Most Popular Movies

What do you already know?
Write down the names of three movies that you like best.
Work with a partner, if you like.

1. _____

2. _____

3. _____

Make predictions
Look at the pictures and headings in the article. Then
write down three things that you think you will learn as
you read this article.

1. _____

2. _____

3. _____

Set your purpose for reading
Write down one thing you hope to find out about the ten
most popular movies of all time as you read this article.

_____

_____

Learn important words
Study the meanings of the words below and how they are
used in sentences. Knowing these words might help you as
you read this article.

setting—where and when a story takes place. *The setting of*
Beverly Hills Cop *changes from Detroit to Los Angeles.*

plot—what happens in a story. *In* Star Wars, *the plot is
about the adventures of Luke Skywalker.*

technology—the use of knowledge to reach a goal.
*Technology is used to produce many special effects in
movies.*

Movies are a medium that everybody seems to enjoy. But teenagers go to movies more than any other group. Almost one-third of the people who go to movies are teenagers, although teenagers make up only about 10 percent of the population. It's not surprising that the most popular movies are ones that teenagers want to see.

Teenage movies

Read the names of the movies on page 129. They are the ten most popular movies of all time. These movies made more money and were seen by more people than any other movies. Notice that all the movies on the list are movies that teenagers liked. Moviemakers have noticed this, too. That's why they make the kinds of movies they do.

All but two of the movies on the list were made in the 1980s. This means that people, especially teenagers, are spending more money for movies than they used to spend. Yet, in some ways, people spend less for movies than in the past. In 1943, about 25 percent of the money that people spent for entertainment was spent at the movies. Today, people spend less than 5 percent of their entertainment money for movies.

Using skills and strategies

Clarifying

As you read, you often read confusing statements. For example, you read that some movies in the 1980s made a record amount of money. You also read that people spend a smaller part of their money for movies today than they used to spend. These two ideas seem to oppose each other. How can movies today make more money if people spend less money for movies?

When you read text that is hard to understand, you need to *clarify*, or explain, the text. Here are two facts that will help you clarify how movies make more money today.

1. Ticket prices for movies are ten times higher today than they were in the 1940s.
2. Fewer movies are made today than were made in the 1940s.

Use these two facts to answer the question: *How can movies today make more money if people spend less money for movies?* Write your answer in the margin.

Simple plots and modern technology

More than half the movies listed have simple plots—the good guys against the bad guys. But moviemakers did something different in these movies. They used the latest technology to create fantastic settings, characters, events, and weapons.

1 E.T. THE EXTRA-TERRESTRIAL (1982)

2 STAR WARS (1977)

3 RETURN OF THE JEDI (1983)

4 THE EMPIRE STRIKES BACK (1980)

5 JAWS (1975)

6 GHOSTBUSTERS (1984)

7 RAIDERS OF THE LOST ARK (1981)

8 INDIANA JONES AND THE TEMPLE OF DOOM (1984)

9 BEVERLY HILLS COP (1984)

10 BACK TO THE FUTURE (1985)

Darth Vader and Luke Skywalker dueled with lightsabers in three different movies on the list. Lightsabers weren't really lasers; they were products of modern technology. The moviemakers covered long glass rods with a special tape. They put motors in the handles of the sabers to turn the rods and make them glow. The light from the sabers was reflected in the camera lens. That made the sabers look even brighter. The blue-white color was put in later with animation.

Using skills and strategies

Clarifying

The text tells you how lightsabers got their color. If you don't know what *animation* is, you need to clarify the meaning of the text. Where would you find the information you need to clarify the text? Write your answer in the margin.

The most popular movie of all time was about a character who was created in a movie laboratory. He looked like a turtle without a shell. He was made of plastic and controlled by motors. His odd-shaped head had huge eyes. A red light

Darth Vader and Luke Skywalker duel with lightsabers in *Return of the Jedi*.

inside his chest went on and off to show how he was feeling. E.T. wasn't a cuddly teddy bear, but everybody loved him.

Not all the ten most popular movies had out-of-this-world characters and settings or fantastic special effects. Not all of them involved good guys and bad guys. In *Back to the Future*, the plot is about a boy who goes back in time. He meets his mother and father as teenagers. There are no battle scenes, no sea monsters, and no ghosts. People loved it. It answered the questions many people have about how their parents acted when they were young.

What kind of movies will be in the theaters next year? To answer this question, think of the movies you and your friends want to see. These are the movies that will be coming soon to a theater near you.

Think About What You've Read

Important ideas
1. How do moviemakers use technology?

_____

2. Which is more important in most very popular movies: plot or special effects? Explain your answer.

_____

_____

3. Which of the ten most popular movies did you like best? Why?

_____

_____

Use what you've learned before

4. How do you think making a movie is both the same as and different from putting newspapers and books together?

_____

_____

_____

Important word meanings

Deadline, editor, plot, technology, and *invention* are words you have learned. Think of a way each word could be used to tell about movie making. Then write a sentence for each word.

_____

_____

_____

Using skills and strategies

Suppose you looked in a dictionary to clarify the meaning of a sentence that uses the word *fantastic*. Which meaning below fits the way *fantastic* is used in the article?

a. unbelievably high. *The price of renting movies has become fantastic.*

b. wild and strange in shape and manner. *Yoda was a fantastic character who taught Luke about life.*

Writing

Choose a movie you saw recently, and write a review for your school newspaper. The movie can be one you saw in a theater or on TV. Tell about the characters, the special effects, and the plot. Make sure you tell your readers if you think the movie is worth spending money to see.

Your important ideas

Look back over the article. Write down one idea that seems to be the most important one to you.

_____

Your important words

Look back at the words you have learned as you read about movies. Write down the word or words that you think are most important—that you would like to remember.

_____

Guglielmo Marconi: Father of Radio

What do you already know?

Write down three things that you already know about how a radio works. Work with a partner, if you like.

1. _____

2. _____

3. _____

Make predictions

Look at the pictures, graphs, tables, and drawings in the article. Also skim the article. Then write down three things that you think you will learn as you read this article.

1. _____

2. _____

3. _____

Set your purpose for reading

Write down one thing you hope to find out about the radio as you read this article.

_____

_____

Learn important words

Study the meanings of the words below and how they are used in sentences. Knowing these words might help you as you read this article.

broadcast—to send out by radio or television. *The radio operator broadcast a call for help.*

experiment—a trial or test to find out something. *Marconi did an experiment to see how far radio waves would travel.*

exist—to be; to be real. *Hertz proved that radio waves exist.*

communication—giving or trading information by speaking or writing. *Radio is a method of communication.*

Radios are a remarkable invention. They're used to broadcast news and music. Police and fire departments use radios to send emergency information. In fact, over a billion radios exist throughout the world. There are 500 million in the United States alone. More than 25,000 radio stations in the world broadcast their signals. Ten thousand of them operate in the United States.

Total Radios in the World

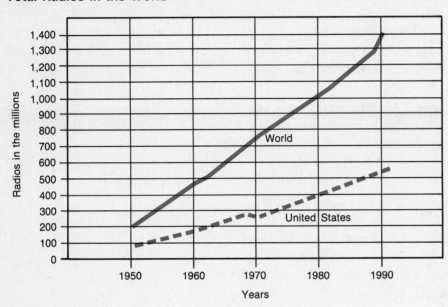

Using skills and strategies

Using pictorial aids

Pictorial aids, such as graphs, pictures, and tables, can help you understand what you read. They often give you information that is not in the text. Sometimes they put the information that is in the text in a new form—one that is easy to understand.

The graph above compares the total number of radios in the world to the number of radios in the United States. The lines go up, showing how the number has grown from 1950 to 1990. Draw a line from the end of each line across to the number to find out how many millions of radios are in use.

The development of the radio

It took almost 75 years to develop radio. Then it took another 75 years to make it better. Like many other inventions, it was the product of the ideas and work of many people. However, we call Guglielmo Marconi the father of radio because he sent the first radio signal through the air.

In Marconi's time, people could send messages to places that were far away. But the messages had to travel over wires. Marconi found a way to send signals without wires.

Early experiments

Marconi was born to a very wealthy family in Italy in 1874. He didn't go to school. He was taught at home by teachers. He was always very interested in science. As he got older, he started doing experiments with electricity.

Electricity was a new field when Marconi was a boy. Many people were studying it. Marconi used his allowance to buy wire and electrical instruments. When his parents wouldn't give him more money to buy equipment, he would sell a pair of his shoes to buy what he needed.

Marconi worked in his laboratory at home. He got books from the teachers at the university. He copied the experiments he found in those books. (You would think that Marconi would have studied at the university. But he failed the entrance exam!)

A teacher at the university showed Marconi the experiments of Heinrich Hertz. Hertz had proved that radio waves exist. In his lab, Hertz connected two coils of wire and two metal balls with a very powerful battery. In another part of the building, he set up a wire ring with two more metal balls. This ring was not connected to the wires in his lab.

Hertz sent electricity through the coil of wire. A spark jumped between the metal balls in both places! Something carried the electricity between the lab and the other part of the building. The carrier became known as radio waves.

The first wireless

The idea occurred to Marconi that Hertz's waves might be used for communication. Marconi set to work on sending and receiving signals. He used the same kind of setup that Hertz had used, but he added a tapping device. He was able to send a signal across his lab. Later, he did the experiment outside. He discovered that if he grounded the wires (connected them to the ground) and added an antenna, he could send a signal one mile. At age 22, Marconi had done what no one else had done: he had broadcast signals through the air without using wire.

Marconi called his invention the wireless radio. He kept trying to make it better. Each time he set it up, he was able to send a signal over a longer distance.

Marconi used Morse code to send messages. This was a system of spelling words with dots and dashes. He improved his radio so that ships could broadcast messages over short distances to other ships and to shore.

Marconi was still not satisfied. He wanted to be able to send the messages farther and farther—perhaps across the Atlantic Ocean! After many tries, he sent his first radio signal across the Atlantic Ocean on December 12, 1901. The signal was the letter *S* in Morse code.

Guglielmo Marconi in 1895

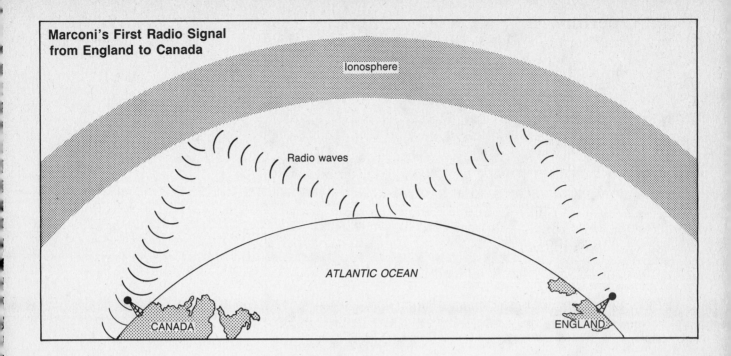

Marconi's First Radio Signal from England to Canada

Ionosphere

Radio waves

ATLANTIC OCEAN

CANADA

ENGLAND

Using skills and strategies

Using pictorial aids

The picture above shows how the signal traveled from England to Canada. Although the article does not tell you, you can see from the picture that radio waves do not move in a straight line. They bounce from the ground up into the sky and back again. What do the radio waves hit above the Earth? Circle its name on the picture.

Over the next three years, Marconi perfected ship-to-ship radio communication. Using wireless radio, messages could travel between ships that were 2,000 miles apart. The success of Marconi's invention made him very rich.

No one realized how important the wireless was until it was used in a terrible sea disaster. In 1912, the radio operator from the *Titanic* sent an SOS to a nearby ship. Over and over he tapped the distress signal (... — — — ...). Although the operator went down with the *Titanic*, his signal brought help that saved over 700 lives.

Many people did more work to develop radio as we know it today. They worked hard on this invention because they realized how important it was. Like other radio pioneers, Marconi spent the rest of his life trying to make his wireless better.

Using skills and strategies

Using pictorial aids

A table can give you a lot of information in a quick way. The table on the next page lists some important dates in the development of radio. Which one took place in your lifetime? Circle it.

Developing Radio

1886 Heinrich Hertz proves the existence of radio waves that move at the speed of light.

1895 Guglielmo Marconi sends the first radio signal through air.

1906 Reginald Fessenden uses radio waves to broadcast his voice.

1920 Radio station WWJ in Detroit becomes the first radio station.

1947 The transistor is developed.

1960 FM stations begin broadcasting in stereo.

1982 AM stations begin broadcasting in stereo.

Think About What You've Read

Important ideas
1. What did Hertz discover?

_____

2. How did Marconi build on Hertz's experiment to send signals across the ocean?

_____

_____

3. How was the wireless radio used to save lives?

_____

_____

4. What kind of person do you think Marconi was? Why?

_____

_____

Use what you've learned before
5. How is radio like newspapers, books, and movies?

_____

_____

_____

Important word meanings

1. What do TV stations **broadcast** in addition to sound?

_____

2. How many radio stations **exist** in the world?

_____

3. Where did Marconi do his first **experiments**?

_____

4. Name two forms of **communication** that use printed pages.

_____

Using skills and strategies

Look at the picture on page 135. Follow the radio signals with your finger and think about what the drawing tells you. Then write what the drawing tells you on the lines below. Use the words in the drawing in your paragraph.

_____

_____

_____

_____

Writing

For one day, keep track of all the time you spend listening to the radio. Make a list of the times and the programs you listen to. Remember to include the times you are doing other things and listening to the radio, too. For example, do you listen while you are getting dressed or doing homework? Use your list to write a paragraph that answers this question: Is radio a big part of your life?

Your important ideas

Look back over the article. Write down one idea that seems to be the most important one to you—the one idea that you would like to remember.

_____

_____

Your important words

Look back at the words you have learned as you read about Marconi. Write down the word or words that you think are most important—that you would like to remember.

_____

_____

Sending a Letter by Telephone

What do you already know?

Write down three things that you already know about how a letter can be copied and sent over the telephone. Work with a partner, if you like.

1. _____
2. _____
3. _____

Make predictions

Look at the pictures in the article. Read the first sentence of each paragraph. Then write down three things that you think you will learn as you read this article.

1. _____
2. _____
3. _____

Set your purpose for reading

Write down one thing you hope to find out about how letters can be sent over the telephone as you read this article.

_____

_____

Learn important words

Study the meanings of the words below and how they are used in sentences. Knowing these words might help you as you read this article.

electric eye—a scanning device that reacts to changes in light. *The electric eye changes light into signals that can be sent over the telephone.*

contract—an agreement in which people agree to do or not do something. *The contract said that the work would be finished by May.*

138

Did you look at the photos on the front page of the paper today? Perhaps there was a picture of a spacecraft landing or the damage caused by a disaster. These events might have happened thousands of miles away from your home. Did you wonder how the newspaper got the photos so quickly?

Not every newspaper has a staff photographer at the site of every news story. The photo of the spacecraft landing or the tornado damage was probably sent to the newspaper over the telephone. "But you can't send pictures through telephone wires," you say. Yes, you can, if you use facsimile, or fax, machines. To fax a picture or a letter, you need two telephones and two fax machines.

Using skills and strategies

Taking notes

You can take notes to help you remember what you read. You don't have to write complete sentences. You can write just a few words. A good time to take notes is after you have read one or two paragraphs. Here are some notes on the first two paragraphs.

can send pictures over telephone
need 2 fax machines and 2 telephones

As you read the next paragraphs, take notes for each paragraph. Write your notes in the margins next to the paragraph.

Here's how a fax machine works. First you dial the telephone number of the person who will be receiving the picture. Then you place the picture on the cylinder of the fax machine that is hooked up to your telephone.

When you turn on your fax machine, the cylinder starts turning. Fax machines use an electric eye to change light into electricity.

The electric eye sends out a tiny beam of light that passes back and forth over the picture as the cylinder turns. The electric eye reads the picture. It then changes the picture into a series of electric signals. These electric signals can go through telephone wires to the fax machine at the other end.

Using skills and strategies

Taking notes

Use the notes you take for the next paragraph to answer the following questions. Write your answers in the margin.
1. Name two parts of a fax machine that help produce a picture.
2. What kind of paper does a fax machine use?

The fax machine on the receiving end turns the electric signals back into the picture. A printer blade and a piece of wire wound around the cylinder do the work. The electric signal passes from the blade to the wire. The electricity in the wire develops the picture on specially treated paper.

Banks, businesses, and government agencies use fax machines to send letters, contracts, drawings, and other materials. Sending materials over the telephone saves time. People can send important messages back and forth without worrying. Messages can't get lost in the mail.

Fax machines have become cheaper over the past few years, so many small businesses can use them. They cost under $1,000 now and are not expensive to use. Each page that is sent costs only the price of a phone call. With a fax machine, people can send messages anywhere in the world in just 15 seconds. You can be sure that you'll be hearing "Just fax it, please" more and more.

Think About What You've Read

Important ideas
1. What is a fax machine?

_____

_____

2. How could you use a fax machine in your home?

_____

_____

3. How could a sports reporter use a fax machine?

_____

_____

_____

Important word meanings

Write three sentences on a separate sheet of paper that tell how a fax machine works. Use the words *communication, electric eye, cylinder,* and *contract* in your sentences.

Using skills and strategies

In the margin, write two or three notes that would help you remember this information.

Many newspaper reporters use telephoto machines to send photos to their offices. These machines work like fax machines, but the pictures are printed out on film instead of on paper. You probably know that film is more sensitive to light than paper is. Newspapers get clearer pictures to print when they use film.

Writing

You've read about several inventions that help people communicate. What do you think will be next? Maybe someone will invent a telephone that lets you "see" who is calling by printing out a picture of the caller. On a sheet of paper, write a paragraph about an invention you think would help people communicate. Tell why the invention is important and how it would be helpful.

Your important ideas

Look back over the article. Write down one idea that seems to be the most important one to you—the one idea that you would like to remember.

_____

_____

Your important words

Look back at the words you have learned as you read this article. Write down the word or words that you think are the most important—that you would like to remember.

_____

_____

Reviewing What You Have Learned

Some facts and ideas you have learned

You learned many important facts and ideas as you read about media. A few of them are listed below. Add your own important ideas to the end of this list. You can look back at the "Your important ideas" section of each lesson to remember the ideas you wrote down.

- A sports reporter sends news about a sports game by computer from the press box to the newspaper office.
- Books used to be made entirely by hand; now they are put together by machines.
- Teenagers like to see movies that feature special effects and fantastic characters.
- Marconi sent the first signal through the air, which led to the development of radio.
- Fax machines can send letters over the telephone.

_____

_____

Some word meanings you have learned

Here are some of the important words you learned in the articles you read. Make sure you understand their meanings. Then add important words of your own. You can look back at the "Your important words" section of each lesson to remember the words you wrote down.

journalism—the work of writing or editing a newspaper, book, or a magazine. *She used to work at a newspaper; now she teaches journalism at a university.*

setting—where and when a story takes place. *The setting of* Back to the Future *is a small town.*

experiment—a trial or test to find out something. *Marconi did his early experiments in a lab at home.*

_____

_____

Purposes for reading

Look back at the section at the beginning of every lesson called "Set your purpose for reading." What purposes did you set for reading the articles in this cluster? Write down one purpose that you achieved. Tell how the article you read helped you meet your purpose.

_____

_____

Using skills and strategies

Reread the first two paragraphs on page 114. On the lines below, write two notes for each paragraph that would help you remember the information. Remember to make your notes brief.

_____

_____

_____

_____

Writing: story

Make a plan for a story that a moviemaker who is famous for special effects might want to use. Include these in your plan: a setting, two or three characters, and one or two details for the plot. Write your story plan on a separate sheet of paper.

Revising

Read your story plan to a classmate. Ask your classmate to suggest changes in the story. Make these changes now. At another time, you might want to write part of the movie you have planned.

Activities

1. Tune your AM radio dial to find stations broadcasting from distant cities. Listen for the stations to identify themselves. Then use a map to find the distance between your city and the station. Compare with your friends to see who found the station that is farthest away. (Hint: Radio signals come in better from distant cities late at night. This is because many smaller stations are off the air at this time.)
2. Look in an encyclopedia or other reference book to find the Morse code. This is the code Marconi used to send his first wireless messages. Practice sending a few simple messages.
3. Be a reporter for a sports event at your school. Include a summary of the game and highlights of some of the important plays in the game.
4. Find out how moviemakers make monsters, such as the shark in _Jaws_. Report to your classmates, telling how the monster was made and how it moved.
5. Do some research in the library to find out how a TV works. Start by looking under _television_ in an encyclopedia.

ACKNOWLEDGMENTS

Photo Credits

Cluster 1: 5: AP/Wide World Photos. **14:** The Bettmann Archive. **20:** UPI/Bettmann Newsphotos. **25:** ©Fredrik D. Bodin/Stock Boston. **28:** AP/Wide World Photos.

Cluster 2: 35: Reuters/Bettmann Newsphotos. **37:** The Bettmann Archive. **39:** UPI/Bettmann Newsphotos. **43:** Culver Pictures. **45:** The Bettmann Archive. **48:** The Bettmann Archive. **49:** The Bettmann Archive. **54:** The Bettmann Archive. **55:** The Bettmann Archive. **59:** ©Ira Kirschenbaum/ Stock Boston. **60:** Marc Deville/Gamma-Liaison. **61:** Thierry Rannou/ Gamma-Liaison.

Cluster 3: 67: ©Len Rue, Jr./Stock Boston. **69:** ©MGM-TV/Movie Still Archives. **73:** Courtesy of The University of Chicago Medical Center/ Wyler Children's Hospital. **74:** ©Peter Vandermark/Stock Boston. **79:** Animals Animals/©L.L. Rue III. **83:** Animals Animals/©Harry Cutting.

Cluster 4: 91: AP/Wide World Photos. **98 (left):** The Bettmann Archive. **98 (right):** Courtesy of Cambridge Instruments Inc., Optical Systems Division. **99 (left):** Courtesy of Centers for Disease Control—Atlanta, Georgia. **99 (right):** Photri/MGA Chicago. **103:** AP/Wide World Photos. **104:** Courtesy of California State Library—California Section. **108:** Marty Snyderman. **109:** Jeff Rotman.

Cluster 5: 115: AP/Wide World Photos. **117:** ©Bob Daemmrich/Stock Boston. **118:** ©Ellis Herwig/Stock Boston. **122:** The Bettmann Archive. **125:** ©Joseph Sterling/TSW—Click Chicago. **130:** ©Twentieth Century-Fox/Movie Still Archives. **134:** The Bettmann Archive. **139:** Courtesy of Fugitsu Imaging Systems of America, Inc.

Illustrators

John T. Carlson, Barbara Corey, Susan C. Mills